Typography is what language looks like.

Dedicated to GEORGE SADEK *and all my teachers*

ELLEN LUPTON

thinking
with

type

A CRITICAL GUIDE
FOR DESIGNERS,
WRITERS, EDITORS,
& STUDENTS

PRINCETON ARCHITECTURAL PRESS · NEW YORK

Published by
Princeton Architectural Press
37 East Seventh Street
New York, New York 10003

For a free catalog of books, call 1.800.722.6657.
Visit our web site at www.papress.com.

Library of Congress Cataloging-in-Publication Data

Lupton, Ellen.
     Thinking with type : a critical guide for
designers, writers, editors, & students /
Ellen Lupton. — 1st ed.
     p. cm. — (Design briefs)
Includes bibliographical references.
ISBN 10: 1-56898-448-0 (alk. paper)
ISBN 13: 978-1-56898-448-3
1. Graphic design (Typography)
2. Type and type-founding.
I. Title. II. Series.

z246.l87 2004
686.2'2—dc22

BOOK DESIGNER
Ellen Lupton

EDITOR
Mark Lamster, Princeton Architectural Press

PROOFREADER
Elizabeth Johnson

COVER DESIGNERS
Jennifer Tobias and Ellen Lupton

DESIGN ASSISTANTS
Eric Karnes and Elke Gasselseder

PHOTOGRAPHER
Dan Meyers

PRIMARY TYPEFACES
Scala, designed by Martin Majoor
Thesis, designed by Lucas de Groot

SPECIAL THANKS TO
Nettie Aljian, Nicola Bednarek, Janet Behning,
Megan Carey, Penny (Yuen Pik) Chu, Russell
Fernandez, Jan Haux, Clare Jacobson, Nancy Eklund
Later, Linda Lee, Katharine Myers, Jane Sheinman,
Scott Tennent, Jennifer Thompson, Joe Weston,
and Deb Wood of Princeton Architectural Press
—Kevin C. Lippert, publisher

CONTENTS

HOOD'S SARSAPARILLA Advertisement, lithograph, 1884
A woman's healthy face bursts through a sheet of text, her bright
complexion proving the product's efficacy better than any written
claim. Both text and image have been drawn by hand, reproduced
via color lithography. Printed here at actual size.

INTRODUCTION

THE ORGANIZATION OF LETTERS on a blank page—or screen—is the designer's most basic challenge. What kind of font to use? How big? How should those letters, words, and paragraphs be aligned, spaced, ordered, shaped, and otherwise manipulated?

Anyone who regularly and enthusiastically commits acts of visual communication will find something to use and enjoy in this book, which offers practical information within a context of design history and theory. Some readers will be chiefly interested in the sections that present basic typographic principles in concise, non-dogmatic layouts. Others will spend more time with the critical essays, which look at the cultural frameworks of typography.

I decided to create this book because there was no adequate text to accompany my own courses in typography, which I have been teaching at Maryland Institute College of Art in Baltimore since 1997. Some books on typography focus on the classical page; others are vast and encyclopedic, overflowing with facts and details. Some rely too heavily on illustrations of their authors' own work, providing narrow views of a diverse practice, while others are chatty and dumbed-down, presented in a condescending tone.

I sought a book that is serene and intelligible, a volume where design and text gently collaborate to enhance understanding. I sought a work that is small and compact, economical yet well constructed—a handbook designed for the hands. I sought a book that reflects the diversity of typographic life, past and present, exposing my students to history, theory, and ideas. Finally, I sought a book that would be relevant across the media of visual communication, from the printed page to the glowing screen.

I had no alternative but to write the book myself.

Thinking with Type is assembled in three sections: LETTER, TEXT, and GRID, building from the basic atom of the letterform to the organization of words into coherent bodies and flexible systems. Each section opens with a narrative essay about the cultural and theoretical issues that fuel typographic design across a range of media. The demonstration pages that follow each essay show not just *how* typography is structured, but *why*, asserting the functional and cultural basis for design habits and conventions.

The first section, LETTER, reveals how early typefaces referred to the body, emulating the work of the hand. The abstractions of neoclassicism bred the strange progeny of nineteenth-century commercial typography. In the twentieth century, avant-garde artists and designers explored the alphabet as a theoretical system. After digital font design became a cottage industry and a mode of underground publishing in the 1980s, typography became a narrative form that revived its connections with the body.

The second section, TEXT, considers the massing of letters into larger bodies. Designers approach text as a continuous field whose grain, color, density, and silhouette can be endlessly adjusted. Technology has shaped the design of typographic space, from the concrete physicality of metal type to the flexibility—and constraints—offered by digital media. Text has evolved from a closed, stable body to a fluid and open ecology.

The third section, GRID, looks at spatial organization. Grids underlie every typographic system. In the early twentieth century, Dada and Futurist artists attacked the rectilinear constraints of metal type and exposed the mechanical grid of letterpress. Swiss designers in the 1940s and 1950s created design's first total methodology by rationalizing the grid. Their work, which introduced programmatic thinking to a field governed by taste and convention, remains profoundly relevant to the systematic thinking required when designing for multimedia.

Throughout the book, examples of design practice demonstrate the elasticity of the typographic system, whose rules can all be broken. Finally, the APPENDIX contains handy lists, helpful hints, dire warnings, and resources for further study.

This book is about thinking *with* typography—in the end, the emphasis falls on *with*. Typography is a tool for doing things *with*: shaping content, giving language a physical body, enabling the social flow of messages. Typography is an ongoing tradition that connects you *with* other designers, past and future. Type is *with* you everywhere you go—the street, the mall, the Web, your apartment. This book aims to speak to, and *with*, all the readers and writers, designers and producers, teachers and students, whose work engages the ordered yet unpredictable life of the visible word.

ACKNOWLEDGMENTS

AS A DESIGNER, WRITER, AND VISUAL THINKER, I am indebted to my teachers at the Cooper Union, where I studied art and design from 1981 to 1985. Back then, the design world was rather neatly divided between a Swiss-inflected modernism and an idea-based approach rooted in American advertising and illustration. My teachers, including George Sadek, William Bevington, and James Craig, staked out an odd place between those worlds, allowing the modernist fascination with abstract systems to collide with the strange, the poetic, and the popular.

The title of this book, *Thinking with Type*, is an homage to James Craig's primer *Designing with Type*, the utilitarian classic that was our text book at Cooper. If that book was a handyman's guide to basic typography, this one is a naturalist's field guide, approaching its subject as an organic system that is more evolutionary than mechanical. What I really learned from my teachers was how to *think* with type: how to use visual and verbal language to develop and deliver ideas. As a student, discovering typography was finding the bridge connecting written language to visual art.

To write my own book for the twenty-first century I have had to educate myself all over again. In 2003 I enrolled in the Doctorate in Communications Design program at the University of Baltimore. There I have worked with Stuart Moulthrop and Nancy Kaplan, world-class scholars, critics, and designers of networked media and digital interfaces. Their influence is seen throughout this book.

My colleagues at Maryland Institute College of Art have built a distinctive design culture at the school; special thanks go to Ray Allen, Fred Lazarus, Elizabeth Nead, Bernard Canniffe, Jennifer Cole Phillips, Rachel Schreiber, and all my students, past and future.

My editor, Mark Lamster, has kept this project alive and conscious across its seemingly endless development. I also thank Eric Karnes and Elke Gasselseder, Kevin Lippert at Princeton Architectural Press, Timothy Linn at Asia Pacific Offset, William Noel at the Walters Art Museum, Paul Warwick Thompson and Barbara Bloemink at the Cooper-Hewitt, National Design Museum, and all the designers who shared their work with me.

I learn something every day from my children, Jay and Ruby, and from my parents, my twin, and the amazing Miller family. My friends—Jennifer Tobias, Edward Bottone, Claudia Matzko, Darsie Alexander, and Joy Hayes—sustain my life. My husband, Abbott Miller, is the greatest designer I know, and I am proud to include him in this volume.

MARTIN MAJOOR *began designing the typeface Seria with this napkin sketch made on a train from Berlin to Warsaw in 1996. The typeface was released by FontShop International in 2000. Most contemporary typefaces ultimately take a digital form, but many are rooted in calligraphic tradition and originate in handwritten sketches and prototypes.*

LETTER

TYPE, SPACES, AND LEADS   3

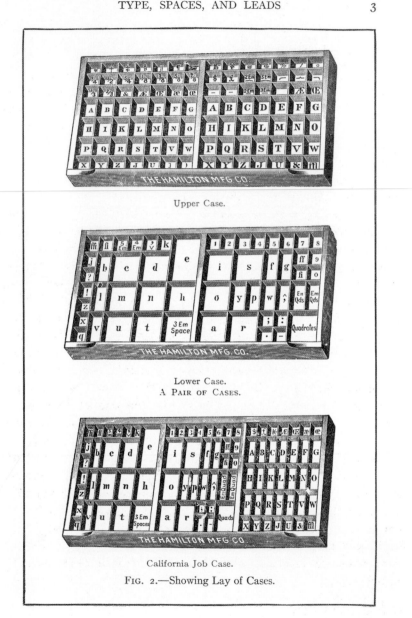

Upper Case.

Lower Case.
A PAIR OF CASES.

California Job Case.
FIG. 2.—Showing Lay of Cases.

TYPE, SPACES, AND LEADS
Diagram from book, 1917
Author: Frank S. Henry
In a traditional printing shop, gridded cases hold fonts of type and spacing material. Capital letters are stored in a drawer above the minuscule letters. Hence the terms "uppercase" and "lowercase" are derived from the physical space of the print shop.

LETTER

THIS IS NOT A BOOK ABOUT FONTS. It is a book about how to use them. Typefaces are an essential resource employed by graphic designers, just as glass, stone, steel, and countless other materials are employed by architects. Graphic designers sometimes create their own fonts and custom lettering. More commonly, however, they tap the vast library of existing typefaces, choosing and combining them in response to a particular audience or situation. To do this with wit and wisdom requires knowledge of how—and why—letterforms have evolved.

Words originated as gestures of the body. The first typefaces were directly modeled on the forms of calligraphy. Typefaces, however, are not bodily gestures—they are manufactured images designed for infinite repetition. The history of typography reflects a continual tension between the hand and the machine, the organic and the geometric, the human body and the abstract system. These tensions, which marked the birth of printed letters over five hundred year ago, continue to energize typography today.

Movable type, invented by Johannes Gutenberg in Germany in the early fifteenth century, revolutionized writing in the West. Whereas scribes had previously manufactured books and documents by hand, printing with type allowed for mass production: large quantities of letters could be cast from a mold and assembled into "forms." After the pages were proofed, corrected, and printed, the letters were put away in gridded cases for reuse.

Movable type had been employed earlier in China, but it had proven less useful there. Whereas the Chinese writing system contains tens of thousands of distinct characters, the Latin alphabet translates the sounds of speech into a small set of marks, making it well-suited to mechanization. Gutenberg's famous Bible took the handmade manuscript as its model. Emulating the dense, dark handwriting known as "blackletter," he reproduced its erratic texture by creating variations of each letter as well as numerous ligatures (characters that combine two or more letters into a single form).

JOHANNES
GUTENBERG
*Printed text,
1456*

This chapter extends and revises "Laws of the Letter," Ellen Lupton and J. Abbott Miller, *Design Writing Research: Writing on Graphic Design* (New York: Kiosk, 1996; London: Phaidon, 1999), 53–61.

NICOLAS JENSON *learned to print in Mainz, the German birthplace of typography, before establishing his own printing press in Venice. His letters have strong vertical stems, and the transition from thick to thin reflects the path of a broad-nibbed pen.*

ilos appellatur mariti
euir dicitur frater mar
ratriæ appellantur qua
mitini fratrum & mat
atrueles matrum fratr
ōſobrini ex duabus ed
ta ſunt in antiquis au

verſe to rekene ¶ Glori
the iiii wekis, and how l
lord, yet the chirche mak
that is to wete, of that he
and of that he cometh to
in thoffyce of the chirc
tynges that ben in this
one partie, & that othe
cause of the comynge of
ben of iove and gladne

GOLDEN TYPE was created by the English design reformer William Morris in 1890. He sought to recapture the dark and solemn density of Jenson's pages.

Lorem ipsum dolor si
consectetuer adipiscing el
Integer pharetra, nisl u
luctus ullamcorper, au
tortor egestas ante, vel
pede urna ac neque. M
ac mi eu purus tincidu

Lorem ipsum dolor sit
consectetuer adipiscing
Integer pharetra, nisl u
luctus ullamcorper, aug
tortor *egestas* ante, vel p
pede urna ac neque. M
ac mi eu purus tincidu

ADOBE JENSON was designed in 1995 by Robert Slimbach, who reconceives historical type-faces for digital use. Adobe Jenson is less mannered and decorative than Centaur.

CENTAUR, designed from 1912 to 114 by Bruce Rogers, is a revival of Jenson's type that emphasizes its ribbonlike stroke.

vanum laboraverunt
si Dominus custodie
stra vigilavit qui cos
num est vobis ante l
rgere postquam sede
i manducatis panem
m dederit dilectis sui
ALMI IVXTA LXX

Lorem ipsum dolor s
consectetuer adipisci
Integer pharetra, nis
ullamcorper, augue t
ante, vel *pharetra* pe
neque. Mauris ac mi
tincidunt faucibus. P
dignissim lectus. Nun

RUIT is designed by the Dutch typographer, teacher, and theorist Gerrit Noordzij. This digitally constructed font, designed in the 1990s, captures the dynamic, three-dimensional quality of fifteenth-century roman typefaces as well as their gothic (rather than humanist) origins. As Noordzij explains, Jenson "adapted the German letters to Italian fashion (somewhat rounder, somewhat lighter), and thus created roman type."

SCALA was introduced in 1991 by the Dutch typographer Martin Majoor. Although this thoroughly contemporary typeface has geometric serifs and rational, almost modular forms, it reflects the calligraphic origins of type, as seen in letters such as a.

HUMANISM AND THE BODY

In fifteenth-century Italy, humanist writers and scholars rejected gothic scripts in favor of the *lettera antica*, a classical mode of handwriting with wider, more open forms. The preference for *lettera antica* was part of the Renaissance (rebirth) of classical art and literature. Nicolas Jenson, a Frenchman who had learned to print in Germany, established an influential printing firm in Venice around 1469. His typefaces merged the gothic traditions he had known in France and Germany with the Italian taste for rounder, lighter forms. They are considered among the first—and finest—roman typefaces.

Many fonts we use today, including Garamond, Bembo, Palatino, and Jenson, are named for printers who worked in the fifteenth and sixteenth centuries. These typefaces are generally known as "humanist." Contemporary revivals of historical fonts are designed to conform with modern technologies and current demands for sharpness and uniformity. Each revival responds to—or reacts against—the production methods, printing styles, and artistic habits of its own time. Some revivals are based on metal types, punches, or drawings that still exist; most rely solely on printed specimens.

Italic letters, also introduced in fifteenth-century Italy (as their name suggests), were modeled on a more casual style of handwriting. While the upright humanist scripts appeared in prestigious, expensively produced books, the cursive form was used by the cheaper writing shops, where it could be written more rapidly than the carefully formed *lettera antica*. Aldus Manutius was a Venetian printer, publisher, and scholar who used italic typefaces in his internationally distributed series of small, inexpensive books. The cursive form saved money because it saved space. Aldus Manutius's books often paired cursive letters with roman capitals; the two styles still were considered fundamentally distinct.

In the sixteenth century, printers began integrating roman and italic forms into type families with matching weights and x-heights (the height of the main body of the lowercase letter). Today, the italic style in most fonts is not simply a slanted version of the roman; it incorporates the curves, angles, and narrower proportions associated with cursive forms.

FRANCESCO
GRIFFO
Roman and italic types designed for Aldus Manutius, c. 1500. They are conceived as two separate typefaces.

JEAN JANNON
Roman and italic types for the Imprimerie Royale, Paris, 1642, coordinated into a larger type family.

comme i'ay des-ia remarqué, ᵃ S. Augu-
ftin demande aux Donatiftes en vne fem-
blable occurrence : *Quoy donc ? lors que
nous lifons , oublions nous comment nous auons
accouftumé de parler ? l'efcriture du grand Dieu*

ᵃ *Aug. lib. 33. contra Fauft. c. 7.* Quid ergo? cum legimus , obliuifcimur quemadmodum loquifoleamus? An fcriptura Dei aliter no-

On the complex origins of roman type, see Gerrit Noordzij, *Letterletter* (Vancouver: Hartley and Marks, 2000).

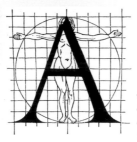

GEOFROY TORY *argued that letters should reflect the ideal human body. Regarding the letter A, he wrote: "the cross-stroke covers the man's organ of generation, to signify that Modesty and Chastity are required, before all else, in those who seek acquaintance with well-shaped letters."*

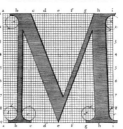

LOUIS SIMONNEAU *designed model letterforms for the printing press of Louis XIV. Instructed by a royal committee, Simonneau designed his letters on a finely meshed grid. A royal typeface (romain du roi) was then created by Philippe Grandjean, based on Simonneau's engravings.*

By WILLIAM CASLON,

ABCD
ABCDE

DOUBL
Quousque t
lina, patient
nos etiam fu
quem ad fin
ABCDEF

WILLIAM CASLON *created typefaces in eighteenth-century England with crisp, upright characters that appear, as Robert Bringhurst has written, "more modelled and less written than Renaissance forms."*

SPECIM

By *JOHN BASKERVILL*

JOHN BASKERVILLE *was a printer working in England in the 1750s and 1760s. He aimed to surpass Caslon by creating sharply detailed letters with more vivid contrast between thick and thin elements. Whereas Caslon's letters were widely used in his own time, Baskerville's work was denounced by many of his contemporaries as amateur and extremist.*

Am indebted to you for two
Letters dated from Corcyra.

*if to me
Country*

AUSTERLITII

GIAMBATTISTA BODONI *created letters at the close of the eighteenth century that exhibit abrupt, unmodulated contrast between thick and thin and razor-thin serifs that are unsupported by curved "brackets." Similar typefaces were designed in the same period by François Ambroise Didot (1784) in France and Justus Erich Walbaum (1800) in Germany.*

A GALLIS

CE

E MAXIN

Aabcdef
ABCD
R

GEORGE BICKHAM, 1743.
Samples of "Roman Print"
and "Italian Hand."

This accusation was reported
to Baskerville in a letter from
his admirer Benjamin
Franklin. For the full letter, see
F. E. Pardoe, *John Baskerville*
of Birmingham: Letter-Founder
and Printer (London: Frederick
Muller Limited, 1975), 68.
See also Robert Bringhurst,
The Elements of Typographic
Style (Vancouver: Hartley and
Marks, 1992, 1997).

ENLIGHTENMENT AND ABSTRACTION

Renaissance artists sought standards of proportion in the idealized human body. The French designer and typographer Geofroy Tory published a series of diagrams in 1529 that linked the anatomy of letters to the anatomy of man. A new approach—distanced from the body—would unfold in the age of scientific and philosophical Enlightenment.

A committee appointed by Louis XIV in France in 1693 set out to construct roman letters against a finely meshed grid. Whereas Geofroy Tory's diagrams were produced as woodcuts, the gridded depictions of the *romain du roi* (king's alphabet) were engraved, made by incising a copper plate with a tool called a graver. The lead typefaces derived from these large-scale diagrams reflect the linear character of engraving as well as the scientific attitude of the king's committee.

Engraved letters—whose fluid lines are unconstrained by letterpress's mechanical grid—offered an apt medium for formal lettering. Engraved reproductions of penmanship disseminated the work of the great eighteenth-century writing masters. Books such as George Bickham's *The Universal Penman* (1743) featured roman letters—each engraved as a unique character—as well as lavishly curved scripts.

Eighteenth-century typography was influenced by new styles of handwriting and their engraved reproductions. Printers like William Caslon in the 1720s and John Baskerville in the 1750s abandoned the rigid nib of humanism for the flexible steel pen and the pointed quill, instruments that rendered a fluid, swelling path. Baskerville, himself a master calligrapher, would have admired the thinly sculpted lines that appeared in the engraved writing books. He created typefaces of such sharpness and contrast that contemporaries accused him of "blinding all the Readers in the Nation; for the strokes of your letters, being too thin and narrow, hurt the Eye." To heighten the startling precision of his pages, Baskerville made his own inks and hot-pressed his pages after printing.

The severe vocabulary of Baskerville was carried to an extreme by Giambattista Bodoni in Italy and Firmin Didot in France at the turn of the nineteenth century. Their typefaces—which have a wholly vertical axis, extreme contrast between thick and thin, and crisp, waferlike serifs—were the gateway to a new vision of typography unhinged from calligraphy.

The *romain du roi* was designed not by a typographer but by a government committee consisting of two priests, an accountant, and an engineer. Robert Bringhurst, 1992

P. VIRGILII MARONIS

BUCOLICA

ECLOGA I. cui nomen *TITYRUS*.

MELIBOEUS, TITYRUS.

Tityre, tu patulæ recubans ſub tegmine fagi
    Silveſtrem tenui Muſam meditaris avena:
Nos patriæ fines, et dulcia linquimus arva;
Nos patriam fugimus: tu, Tityre, lentus in umbra
5 Formoſam reſonare doces Amaryllida ſilvas.

    T. O Meliboee, Deus nobis hæc otia fecit:
Namque erit ille mihi ſemper Deus: illius aram
Sæpe tener noſtris ab ovilibus imbuet agnus.
Ille meas errare boves, ut cernis, et ipſum
10 Ludere, quæ vellem, calamo permiſit agreſti.

    M. Non equidem invideo; miror magis: undique totis
Uſque adeo turbatur agris. en ipſe capellas
Protenus æger ago: hanc etiam vix, Tityre, duco:
Hic inter denſas corylos modo namque gemellos,
15 Spem gregis, ah! ſilice in nuda connixa reliquit.
Sæpe malum hoc nobis, ſi mens non læva fuiſſet,
De coelo taĉtas memini prædicere quercus:
Sæpe ſiniſtra cava prædixit ab ilice cornix.
Sed tamen, iſte Deus qui ſit, da, Tityre, nobis.

20   *T.* Urbem, quam dicunt Romam, Meliboee, putavi
Stultus ego huic noſtræ ſimilem, quo ſæpe ſolemus
Paſtores ovium teneros depellere foetus.
Sic canibus catulos ſimiles, ſic matribus hoedos

A

Noram;

VIRGIL (LEFT)
Book page, 1757
Printed by John Baskerville
The typefaces created by John Baskerville in the eighteenth century were remarkable— even shocking—in their day for their sharp, upright forms and stark contrast between thick and thin elements. In addition to a roman text face, this page utilizes italic capitals, large-scale capitals (generously letterspaced), small capitals (scaled to coordinate with lowercase text), and non-lining or old-style numerals (designed with ascenders, descenders, and a small body height to work with lowercase characters).

RACINE (RIGHT)
Book page, 1801
Printed by Firmin Didot
The typefaces cut by the Didot family in France were even more abstract and severe than those of Baskerville, with slablike, unbracketed serifs and a stark contrast from thick to thin. Nineteenth-century printers and typographers called these glittering typefaces "modern."

Both pages are reproduced from William Dana Orcutt, In Quest of the Perfect Book (New York: Little, Brown and Company, 1926); margins are not accurate.

LA THÉBAÏDE,

OU

LES FRERES ENNEMIS,

TRAGÉDIE.

ACTE PREMIER.

SCENE I.

JOCASTE, OLYMPE.

JOCASTE.

ILS sont sortis, Olympe? Ah! mortelles douleurs!
Qu'un moment de repos me va coûter de pleurs!
Mes yeux depuis six mois étoient ouverts aux larmes,
Et le sommeil les ferme en de telles alarmes!
Puisse plutôt la mort les fermer pour jamaïs,
Et m'empêcher de voir le plus noir des forfaits!
Mais en sont-ils aux mains?

1825;
At 10 o'Clock in the Morning:

A QUANTITY OF OL

ORDAG

Sails &c

ing the rema

ck of the Sch

[J. Soulb

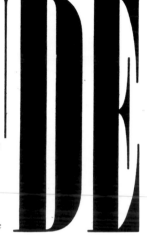

FAT FACE *is the name that was given to the inflated, hyper-bold type style introduced in the early nineteenth century. These faces exaggerated the polarization of letters into thick and thin components seen in the formal typography of Bodoni and Didot.*

EXTRA CONDENSED *typefaces are designed to fit in narrow spaces. Nineteenth-century advertisements often combined fonts of varying style and proportion on a single page. These bombastic mixtures were typically aligned, however, in static, centered compositions.*

EGYPTIAN, *or slab, typefaces transformed the serif from a refined detail to a load-bearing slab. As an independent architectural component, the slab serif asserts its own weight and mass. Introduced in 1806, this style was quickly denounced by purists as "a typographical monstrosity."*

GOTHIC *is a nineteenth-century term for letters with no serifs. Such typefaces could command attention with their massive frontality. Although sans-serif fonts often served in the twentieth century to convey neutrality, flamboyantly decorated gothics were once common.*

**My person was hideous, my stature gigantic. What did this mean? Who was I? What was I?...
Accursed creator! Why did you create a monster so hideous that even you turned away from
me in disgust?** Mary Shelley, *Frankenstein*, 1831

MONSTER FONTS

Although Bodoni and Didot fueled their designs with the calligraphic practices of their time, they created forms that collided with typographic tradition and unleashed a strange new world, where the structural attributes of the letter—serif and stem, thick and thin strokes, vertical and horizontal stress—would be subject to bizarre experiments. In search of a beauty both rational and sublime, Bodoni and Didot had created a monster: an abstract and dehumanized approach to the design of letters.

With the rise of industrialization and mass consumption in the nineteenth century came the explosion of advertising, a new form of communication demanding new kinds of typography. Big, bold faces were designed by distorting the anatomical elements of classical letters. Fonts of astonishing height, width, and depth appeared—expanded, contracted, shadowed, inlined, fattened, faceted, and floriated. Serifs abandoned their role as finishing details to become independent architectural structures, and the vertical stress of traditional letters migrated in new directions.

| ANTIQUE | CLARENDON | LATIN/ANTIQUE TUSCAN | TUSCAN |

Type historian Rob Roy Kelly (1926–2004) studied the mechanized design strategies that served to generate a spectacular variety of display letters in the nineteenth century. This diagram shows how the basic square serif form—called Egyptian or slab—was cut, pinched, pulled, and curled to spawn new species of ornament. Serifs were transformed from calligraphic end-strokes into independent geometric elements that could be freely adjusted.

Lead, the material for casting metal type, is too soft to hold its shape at large sizes under the pressure of the printing press. In contrast, type cut from wood could be printed at gigantic scales. The introduction of the combined pantograph and router in 1834 revolutionized wood-type manufacture. The pantograph is a tracing device that, when linked to a router for carving, allows a parent drawing to spawn variants with different proportions, weights, and decorative excrescences.

This mechanized design approach treated the alphabet as a flexible system divorced from the calligraphic tradition. The search for archetypal, perfectly proportioned letterforms gave way to a view of typography as an elastic system of formal features (weight, stress, stem, crossbars, serifs, angles, curves, ascenders, descenders). The relationships among letters in a font became more important than the identity of individual characters.

For extensive analysis and examples of decorated types, see Rob Roy Kelly, *American Wood Type: 1828–1900, Notes on the Evolution of Decorated and Large Letters* (New York: Da Capo Press, 1969). See also Ruari McLean, "An Examination of Egyptians," *Texts on Type: Critical Writings on Typography*, ed. Steven Heller and Philip B. Meggs (New York: Allworth Press, 2001), 70–76.

DURYEA'S IMPORTED
CORNSTARCH (LEFT)
Lithographic trade card, 1878
*The rise of advertising in the
nineteenth century stimulated
demand for large-scale letters that
could command attention in
urban space. Here, a man is
shown posting a bill in flagrant
disregard for the law, while a
police officer approaches from
around the corner.*

FULL MOON (RIGHT)
Letterpress poster, 1875
*A dozen different fonts are used
in this poster for a steamship
cruise. A size and style of typeface
has been chosen for each line to
maximize the scale of the letters
in the space allotted. Although
the typefaces are exotic, the
centered layout is as static and
conventional as a tombstone.*

FULL MOON.

ST. MICHAEL'S
TEMPERANCE BAND !

Prof. V. Yeager, Leader, will give a

GRAND
MOONLIGHT
EXCURSION

On the Steamer

BELLE !

To Osbrook and Watch Hill,
On Saturday Evening, July 17th,

Leaving Wharf at 7½ o'clock. Returning to Westerly at 10½ o'clock. Kenneth will be at Osbrook.

TICKETS, - FORTY CENTS.

G. B. & J. H. Utter, Steam Printers, Westerly, R. I.

THEO VAN DOESBURG, *founder and chief promoter of the Dutch De Stijl movement, designed this alphabet with perpendicular elements in 1919. Applied here to the letterhead of the Union of Revolutionary Socialists, the hand-drawn characters vary in width, allowing them to fill out the overall rectangle. The De Stijl movement called for the reduction of painting, architecture, objects, and letters to elemental units.*

BOND VAN REVOLUTIONNAIR SOCIALISTISCHE INTELLECTUEELEN

DE STIJL

VILMOS HUSZÁR *designed this logo for the magazine De Stijl in 1917. Whereas Van Doesburg's characters are unbroken, Huszár's letters consist of pixel-like modules.*

abcdefghi jklmnopqr s tuvwxyz a   d d

HERBERT BAYER *created this typeface design, called universal, at the Bauhaus in 1925. Consisting only of lowercase letters, it is built from straight lines and circles.*

FETTE FUTURA

GOETH STOFF

PAUL RENNER *designed Futura in Germany in 1927. Although it is strongly geometric, with perfectly round Os, Futura is a practical, subtly designed typeface that remains widely used today.*

REFORM AND REVOLUTION

EDWARD JOHNSTON *based this 1906 diagram of "essential" characters on ancient Roman inscriptions. While deriding commercial display lettering, Johnston accepted the embellishment of medieval-inspired forms.*

On Futura, see Christopher Burke, *Paul Renner: The Art of Typography* (New York: Princeton Architectural Press, 1998). On the experimental typefaces of the 1920s and 1930s, see Robin Kinross, *Unjustified Texts: Perspectives on Typography* (London: Hyphen Press, 2002), 233–45.

Some designers viewed the distortion of the alphabet as gross and immoral, tied to a destructive and inhumane industrial system. Writing in 1906, Edward Johnston revived the search for an essential, standard alphabet and warned against the "dangers" of exaggeration. Johnston, inspired by the nineteenth-century Arts and Crafts movement, looked back to the Renaissance and Middle Ages for pure, uncorrupted letterforms.

Although reformers like Johnston remained romantically attached to history, they redefined the designer as an intellectual distanced from the commercial mainstream. The modern design reformer was a critic of society, striving to create objects and images that would challenge and revise dominant habits and practices.

The avant-garde artists of the early twentieth century rejected historical forms but adopted the model of the critical outsider. Members of the De Stijl group in the Netherlands reduced the alphabet to perpendicular elements. At the Bauhaus, Herbert Bayer and Josef Albers constructed alphabets from basic geometric forms—the circle, square, and triangle—which they viewed as elements of a universal language of vision.

Such experiments approached the alphabet as a system of abstract relationships. Like the popular printers of the nineteenth century, avant-garde designers abandoned the quest for an essential, perfectly shaped alphabet, but they offered austere, theoretical alternatives in place of the solicitous novelty of mainstream advertising.

Assembled, like machines, from modular components, these experimental designs emulated factory production. Yet most were produced by hand rather than as mechanical typefaces (although many are now available digitally). Futura, designed by Paul Renner in 1927, embodied the obsessions of the avant garde in a multipurpose, commercially available typeface. Although Renner rejected the active movement of calligraphy in favor of forms that are "calming" and abstract, he tempered the geometry of Futura with subtle variations in stroke, curve, and proportion. Renner designed Futura in numerous weights, viewing his font as a painterly tool for constructing a page in shades of gray.

The calming, abstract forms of those new typefaces that dispense with handwritten movement offer the typographer new shapes of tonal value that are very purely attuned. These types can be used in light, semi-bold, or in saturated black forms. Paul Renner, 1931

neu
alphabet

a possibility for the new development

een mogelijkheid voor de nieuwe ontwikkeling

une possibilité pour le développement nouveau

eine möglichkeit für die neue entwicklung

an introduction for a programmed typography

WIM CROUWEL *published his designs for a "new alphabet," consisting of no diagonals or curves, in 1967. The Foundry (London) began developing and releasing digital editions of Crouwel's typefaces in 1997.*

See Wim Crouwel, *New Alphabet* (Amsterdam: Wim Crouwel/Total Design, 1967); and Wim Crouwel, Kees Broos, and David Quay, *Wim Crouwel: Alphabets* (Amsterdam: BIS Publishers, 2003).

TYPE AS PROGRAM

Responding in 1967 to the rise of electronic communication, the Dutch designer Wim Crouwel published designs for a "new alphabet" constructed from straight lines. Rejecting centuries of typographic convention, he designed his letters for optimal display on a video screen (CRT), where curves and angles are rendered with horizontal scan lines. In a brochure promoting his new alphabet, subtitled "An Introduction for a Programmed Typography," he proposed a design methodology in which decisions are rule-based and systematic.

WIM CROUWEL presented this "scanned" version of a Garamond a in contrast with his own new alphabet, whose forms accept the gridded structure of the screen.

In the mid-1980s, personal computers and low-resolution printers put the tools of typography in the hands of a broader public. In 1985 Zuzana Licko began designing typefaces that exploited the rough grain of early desktop systems. While other digital fonts imposed the coarse grid of screen displays and dot-matrix printers onto traditional typographic forms, Licko embraced the language of digital equipment. She and her husband, Rudy VanderLans, cofounders of Emigre Fonts and *Emigre* magazine, called themselves the "new primitives," pioneers of a technological dawn.

ZUZANA LICKO created coarse-resolution fonts for desktop screens and printers in 1985. These fonts have since been integrated into Emigre's extensive Lo-Res font family, designed for print and digital media.

See Rudy VanderLans and Zuzana Licko, *Emigre: Graphic Design into the Digital Realm* (New York: Van Nostrand Reinhold, 1993).

By the early 1990s, with the introduction of high-resolution laser printers and outline font technologies such as PostScript, type designers were less constrained by low-resolution outputs. The rise of the Internet as well as cell phones, hand-held video games, and PDAs, have insured the continued relevance of pixel-based fonts as more and more information is designed for publication directly on screen.

Living with computers gives funny ideas. Wim Crouwel, 1967

CURATOR : JOSEPH WESNER
Linda Ferguson

Steve Handschu
James Hay

Matthew Holland SCULPTURE
Gary Laatsch
Brian Liljeblad
Dora Natella
Matthew Schellenberg
Richard String

Michell Thomas

Robert Wilhelm

Opening Reception : Friday June 8, 5:30—8:30 pm

SCULPTURE

JUNE 8—JULY 7, 1990

ED FELLA *produced a body of experimental typography that strongly influenced typeface design in the 1990s. His posters for the Detroit Focus Gallery feature damaged and defective forms, drawn by hand or culled from third-generation photocopies or from sheets of transfer lettering. Collection of the Cooper-Hewitt, National Design Museum.*

Detroit Focus Gallery (313) 962 -90 2 5
743 Beaubien, Third Floor
DETROIT, MICHIGAN 48226
WEDNESDAY · SATURDAY
Hours: Noon to 6 pm

ALSO IN THE AREA: THE MARKET PRESENTS Peter Gilleran · Gordon Orear Opening 5 · 7:30 pm. Friday, June 8.

TYPE AS NARRATIVE

In the early 1990s, as digital design tools began supporting the seamless reproduction and integration of media, many designers grew dissatisfied with clean, unsullied surfaces, seeking instead to plunge the letter into the harsh and caustic world of physical processes. Letters, which for centuries had sought perfection in ever more exact technologies, became scratched, bent, bruised, and polluted.

Template Gothic: flawed technology

Barry Deck's typeface Template Gothic, designed in 1990, is based on letters drawn with a plastic stencil. The typeface thus refers to a process that is at once mechanical and manual. Deck designed Template Gothic while he was a student of Ed Fella, whose experimental posters inspired a generation of digital typographers. After Template Gothic was released commercially by Emigre Fonts, its use spread worldwide, making it an emblem of "digital typography" for the 1990s.

Dead History: feeding on the past

P. Scott Makela's typeface Dead History, also designed in 1990, is a pastiche of two existing typefaces: the traditional serif font Centennial and the Pop classic VAG Rounded. By manipulating the vectors of readymade fonts, Makela adopted the sampling strategy employed in contemporary art and music. He also referred to the importance of history and precedent, which play a role in nearly every typographic innovation.

CcDdEeFfGgHhIiJjKk

The Dutch typographers Erik von Blokland and Just van Rossum have combined the roles of designer and programmer, creating typefaces that embrace chance, change, and uncertainty. Their 1990 typeface Beowulf was the first in a series of typefaces with randomized outlines and programmed behaviors.

The industrial methods of producing typography meant that all letters had to be identical....Typography is now produced with sophisticated equipment that doesn't impose such rules. The only limitations are in our expectations. Erik van Blokland and Just van Rossum, 2000

BACK TO WORK

Although the 1990s are best remembered for images of decay, typeface designers continued to build a repertoire of general purpose fonts designed to comfortably accommodate broad bodies of text. Rather than narrate the story of their own birth, such workhorse fonts provide graphic designers with flexible palettes of letterforms coordinated within larger families.

Mrs Eaves: working woman

Zuzana Licko, fearless pioneer of the digital dawn, produced historical revivals during the 1990s alongside her experimental display faces. Her 1996 typeface Mrs Eaves, inspired by the eighteenth-century types of John Baskerville (and named after his mistress and housekeeper Sarah Eaves), became one of the most popular typefaces of its time.

Quadraat: all-purpose Baroque

Designed in the Netherlands, typefaces such as Martin Majoor's Scala (used for the text of this book) and Fred Smeijers's Quadraat offer crisp interpretations of typographic tradition. These typefaces look back to sixteenth-century printing from a contemporary point of view, as seen in their decisively geometric serifs. Introduced in 1992, the Quadraat family has expanded to include sans-serif forms in numerous weights and styles.

Gotham: blue-collar curves

In 2000 Tobias Frere-Jones introduced Gotham, derived from letters found at the Port Authority Bus Terminal in New York City. Gotham expresses a no-nonsense, utilitarian attitude that persists today alongside the aesthetics of grunge, neofuturism, pop-culture parodies, and straight historical revivals that are all part of contemporary typography.

When choosing a font, graphic designers consider the history of typefaces and their current connotations as well as their formal qualities. The goal is to find an appropriate match between a style of letters and the specific social situation and body of content that define the project at hand. There is no playbook that assigns a fixed meaning or function to every typeface; each designer must confront the library of possibilities in light of a project's unique circumstances.

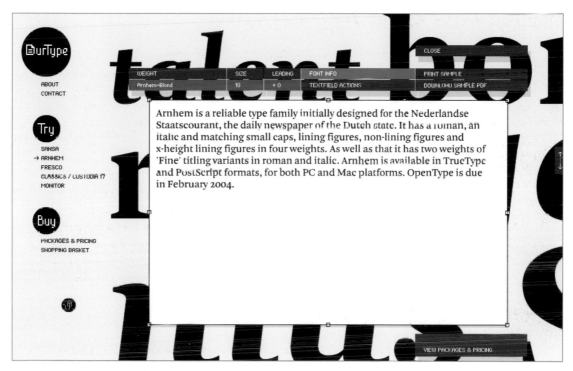

OURTYPE.COM
Web site, 2004
Designers and publishers: Fred
Smeijers and Rudy Geeraerts
*This Flash-based Web site for a
digital type foundry allows users
to test fonts on the fly. The designers
launched their own "label" after
creating fonts such as Quadraat
for FontShop International.
Displayed here is the typeface
Arnhem.*

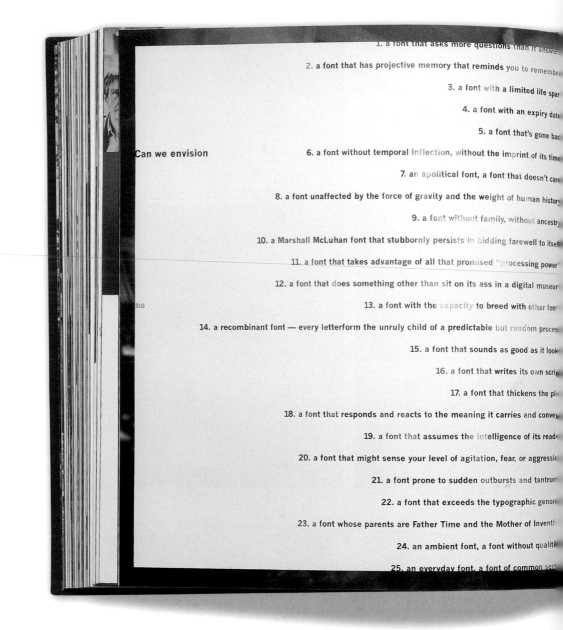

1. a font that asks more questions than it answers

2. a font that has projective memory that reminds you to remember

3. a font with a limited life span

4. a font with an expiry date

5. a font that's gone bad

Can we envision

6. a font without temporal inflection, without the imprint of its time

7. an apolitical font, a font that doesn't care

8. a font unaffected by the force of gravity and the weight of human history

9. a font without family, without ancestry

10. a Marshall McLuhan font that stubbornly persists in bidding farewell to itself

11. a font that takes advantage of all that promised "processing power"

12. a font that does something other than sit on its ass in a digital museum

310

13. a font with the capacity to breed with other fonts

14. a recombinant font — every letterform the unruly child of a predictable but random process

15. a font that sounds as good as it looks

16. a font that writes its own script

17. a font that thickens the plot

18. a font that responds and reacts to the meaning it carries and conveys

19. a font that assumes the intelligence of its reader

20. a font that might sense your level of agitation, fear, or aggression

21. a font prone to sudden outbursts and tantrums

22. a font that exceeds the typographic genome

23. a font whose parents are Father Time and the Mother of Invention

24. an ambient font, a font without qualities

25. an everyday font, a font of common sense

26. a font that slows the pace of reading for the difficult passages (and skips along through easy bits)

27. a font that writes between the lines

28. a font that refuses to utter imperatives or commands

29. a karaoke font, a lip-synching font, a font without a voice of its own

30. a font that listens while it speaks

31. a font that toggles effortlessly between languages

32. a font for speaking in tongues

33. a font that speaks in dialects

34. a metropolitan font for uptown, the ghetto, and suburbia alike

35. a font that simultaneously translates

36. a font that sings the plaintive songs of lonely whales

37. a font that grows

38. a font that learns

39. an evolutionary font

40. an entropic font

41. a "live" font

42. a promiscuous font, a font that fucks fonts, a font-fucking-font

43. a font that emerges, unfolds, performs, evolves, and passes away

44. a font of youth

45. twin fonts, identical but distinct

46. a generative font that renders itself according to behavioral tendencies

47. a font that is something other than a recording

48. a font that is different every time you "play" it

49. a font with the metabolism of a fly

50. a font with a demographic algorithm that projects itself onto you, the average reader

LIFE STYLE
Book, 2000
Designer and author: Bruce Mau
Publisher: Phaidon
Photograph: Dan Meyers

In this post-industrial manifesto, graphic designer Bruce Mau imagines a typeface that comes alive with simulated intelligence.

Some elements may extend slightly above the cap height.

CAP HEIGHT *is the distance from the baseline to the top of capital letter. The cap height of a typeface determines its point size.*

skin, Bones

X-HEIGHT *is the height of the main body of the lowercase letter (or the height of a lowercase x), excluding its ascenders and descenders.*

THE BASELINE *is where all the letters sit. This is the most stable axis along a line of text, and it is a crucial edge for aligning text with images or with other text.*

The curves at the bottom of letters such as o or e hang slightly below the baseline. Commas and semicolons also cross the baseline. If a typeface were not positioned this way, it would appear to teeter precariously, lacking a sense of physical grounding.

body

Although kids learn to write using ruled paper that divides letters exactly in half, most typefaces are not designed that way. The x-height usually occupies slightly more than half of the cap height. The bigger the x-height is in relation to the cap height, the bigger the letters will look. In a field of text, the greatest density occurs between the baseline and the top of the x-height.

Hey, look!
They supersized
my x-height.

Two blocks of text are often aligned along a shared baseline. Here, 14/18 Scala (14-pt type with 18 pts of line spacing) is paired with 7/9 Scala.

12 points
equal 1 pica

6 picas
(72 points)
equal 1 inch

60-POINT SCALA
*A typeface is measured
from the top of the
capital letter to the
bottom of the lowest
descender, plus a small
buffer space.*

*In metal type,
the point size
is the height of
the type slug.*

HEIGHT Attempts to standardize the measurement of type began in the eighteenth century. The *point system,* used to measure the height of a letter as well as the distance between lines (*leading*), is the standard used today. One *point* equals 1/72 inch or .35 millimeters. Twelve points equal one *pica,* the unit commonly used to measure column widths.

Typography also can be measured in inches, millimeters, or pixels. Most software applications let the designer choose a preferred unit of measure; picas and points are a standard default.

ABBREVIATING PICAS AND POINTS

8 picas = 8p

8 points = p8, 8 pts

8 picas, 4 points = 8p4

8-point Helvetica with 9 points of line spacing = 8/9 Helvetica

WIDE LOAD

INTERSTATE BLACK
The set width is the body of the letter plus the space beside it.

TIGHT WAD

INTERSTATE BLACK COMPRESSED
The letters in the condensed version of the typeface have a narrower set width.

WIDE LOAD

TIGHT WAD

TYPE CRIME:
HORIZONTAL & VERTICAL SCALING
The proportions of the letters have been digitally distorted in order to create wider or narrower letters.

WIDTH A letter also has a horizontal measure, called its *set width.* The set width is the body of the letter plus a sliver of space that protects it from other letters. The width of a letter is intrinsic to the proportion of the typeface. Some typefaces have a narrow set width, and some have a wide one.

You can change the set width of a typeface by fiddling with its horizontal or vertical scale. This distorts the proportion of the letters, forcing heavy elements to become thin, and thin elements to become thick. Instead of torturing a letterform, choose a typeface with the proportions you need, such as condensed, compressed, or extended.

Do I **look fat** in this paragraph?

These letters are all the same point size, but they have different x-heights, line weights, and proportions.

When two typefaces are set in the same point size, one often looks bigger than the other. Differences in x-height, line weight, and character width affect the letters' apparent scale.

Mrs Eaves, designed by Zuzana Licko in 1996, rejects the twentieth-century appetite for supersized x-heights. The font, inspired by the eighteenth-century designs of John Baskerville, is named after Sarah Eaves, Baskerville's mistress, housekeeper, and collaborator. The couple lived together for sixteen years before marrying in 1764.

nice *x*-height

48-PT HELVETICA   48-PT MRS EAVES

Bigger x-heights, introduced in the twentieth century, make fonts look larger by maximizing the area within the overall point size.

Every typeface wants to know, "Do I look fat in this paragraph?" It's all a matter of context. A font could look perfectly sleek on screen, yet appear bulky and out of shape in print. Some typefaces are drawn with heavier lines than others, or they have taller x-heights. Helvetica isn't fat. She has big bones.

9/12 HELVETICA

Every typeface wants to know, "Do I look fat in this paragraph?" It's all a matter of context. A font could look perfectly sleek on screen, yet appear bulky and out of shape in print.

12/14 HELVETICA

Every typeface wants to know, "Do I look fat in this paragraph?" It's all a matter of context. A font could look perfectly sleek on screen, yet appear bulky and out of shape in print. Some typefaces are drawn with heavier lines than others or have taller x-heights. Mrs Eaves has a low waist and a small body.

9/12 MRS EAVES

Every typeface wants to know: "Do I look fat in this paragraph?" It's all a matter of context. A font could look perfectly sleek on screen, yet appear bulky and out of shape in print. Mrs. Eaves has a low waist and a small body.

12/14 MRS EAVES

The default type size in many software applications is 12 pts. Although this generally creates readable type on screen displays, 12-pt text type usually looks big and horsey on a printed page. (12 pts is a good size for children's books.) Sizes between 9 and 11 pts are common for printed text. This caption is 7.5 pts.

die schä-
del
knacken
hören

42

REVOLVER.
ZEITSCHRIFT FÜR FILM
(MAGAZINE FOR FILM)
Magazine, 1998–2003
Designer: Gerwin Schmidt
*This magazine is created by and
for film directors. The contrast
between the big type and the small
pages creates drama and surprise.*

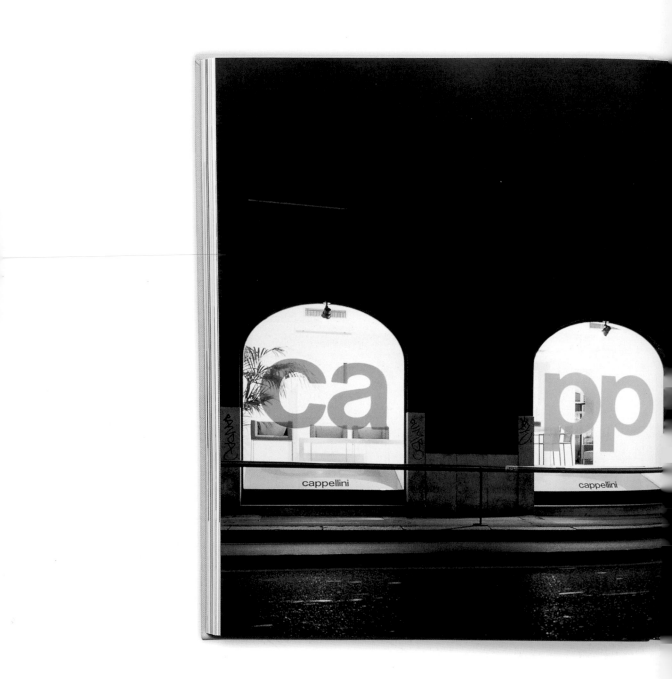

JASPER MORRISON:
EVERYTHING BUT THE WALLS
Book, 2002
Book designers: Jasper
Morrison, Lars Müller,
Matilda Plöjel
Publisher: Lars Müller
Cappellini store windows
designed by Jasper Morrison
Photograph: Dan Meyers
*Typography is realized at an
urban scale in this storefront
created by the industrial designer
Jasper Morrison. The existing
architecture determines the size
and pacing of the monumental
letters.*

SABON

BASKERVILLE

BODONI

HUMANIST OR OLD STYLE
The roman typefaces of the fifteenth and sixteenth centuries emulated classical calligraphy. Sabon was designed by Jan Tschichold in 1966, based on the sixteenth-century typefaces of Claude Garamond.

TRANSITIONAL
These typefaces have sharper serifs and a more vertical axis than humanist letters. When the fonts of John Baskerville were introduced in the mid-eighteenth century, their sharp forms and high contrast were considered shocking.

MODERN
The typefaces designed by Giambattista Bodoni in the late eighteenth and early nineteenth centuries are radically abstract. Note the thin, straight serifs; vertical axis; and sharp contrast from thick to thin strokes.

TYPE CLASSIFICATION A basic system for classifying typefaces was devised in the nineteenth century, when printers sought to identify a heritage for their own craft analogous to that of art history. *Humanist* letterforms are closely connected to calligraphy and the movement of the hand. *Transitional* and *modern* typefaces are more abstract and less organic. These three main groups correspond roughly to the Renaissance, Baroque, and Enlightenment periods in art and literature. Historians and critics of typography have since proposed more finely grained schemes that attempt to better capture the diversity of letterforms. Designers in the twentieth and twenty-first centuries have continued to create new typefaces based on historic characteristics.

CLARENDON

EGYPTIAN OR SLAB SERIF
Numerous bold and decorative typefaces were introduced in the nineteenth century for use in advertising. Egyptian fonts have heavy, slablike serifs.

GILL SANS

HELVETICA

FUTURA

HUMANIST SANS SERIF
Sans-serif typefaces became common in the twentieth century. Gill Sans, designed by Eric Gill in 1928, has humanist characteristics. Note the small, lilting counter in the letter a, and the calligraphic variations in line weight.

TRANSITIONAL SANS SERIF
Helvetica, designed by Max Miedinger in 1957, is one of the world's most widely used typefaces. Its uniform, upright character makes it similar to transitional serif letters. These fonts are also referred to as "anonymous sans serif."

GEOMETRIC SANS SERIF
Some sans-serif types are built around geometric forms. In Futura, designed by Paul Renner in 1927, the Os are perfect circles, and the peaks of the A and M are sharp triangles.

Sabon
14-PT SABON

This is not a book about fonts. It is a book about how to use them. Typefaces are essential resources for the graphic designer, just as glass, stone, steel, and other materials are employed by the architect.

9/12 SABON

Selecting type with wit and wisdom requires knowledge of how and why letterforms evolved.

7/9

Baskerville
14-PT BASKERVILLE

This is not a book about fonts. It is a book about how to use them. Typefaces are essential resources for the graphic designer, just as glass, stone, steel, and other materials are employed by the architect.

9/12 BASKERVILLE

Selecting type with wit and wisdom requires knowledge of how and why letterforms evolved.

7/9

Bodoni
14-PT BODONI

This is not a book about fonts. It is a book about how to use them. Typefaces are essential resources for the graphic designer, just as glass, stone, steel, and other materials are employed by the architect.

9.5/12 BODONI BOOK

Selecting type with wit and wisdom requires knowledge of how and why letterforms evolved.

7.5/9

Clarendon
14-PT CLARENDON
LIGHT

This is not a book about fonts. It is a book about how to use them. Typefaces are essential resources for the graphic designer, just as glass, stone, steel, and other materials are employed by the architect.

8/12 CLARENDON LIGHT

Selecting type with wit and wisdom requires knowledge of how and why letterforms evolved.

6/9

Gill Sans
14-PT GILL SANS

This is not a book about fonts. It is a book about how to use them. Typefaces are essential resources for the graphic designer, just as glass, stone, steel, and other materials are employed by the architect.

9/12 GILL SANS REGULAR

Selecting type with wit and wisdom requires knowledge of how and why letterforms evolved.

7/9

Helvetica
14-PT HELVETICA

This is not a book about fonts. It is a book about how to use them. Typefaces are essential resources for the graphic designer, just as glass, stone, steel, and other materials are employed by the architect.

8/12 HELVETICA REGULAR

Selecting type with wit and wisdom requires knowledge of how and why letterforms evolved.

6/9

Futura
14-PT FUTURA

This is not a book about fonts. It is a book about how to use them. Typefaces are essential resources for the graphic designer, just as glass, stone, steel, and other materials are employed by the architect.

8.5/12 FUTURA BOOK

Selecting type with wit and wisdom requires knowledge of how and why letterforms evolved.

6.5/9

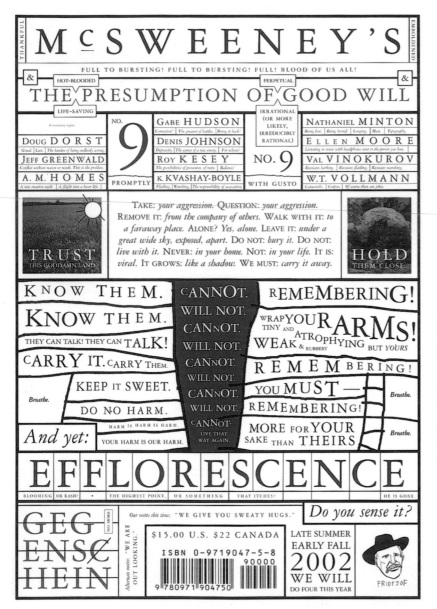

Adobe Garamond was designed by Robert Slimbach in 1988.

The idea of organizing typefaces into matched *families* dates back to the sixteenth century, when printers began coordinating roman and italic faces. The concept was formalized at the turn of the twentieth century.

The roman font is the core or spine from which a family of typefaces derives.

ADOBE GARAMOND REGULAR

The roman form, also called "plain" or "regular," is the standard, upright version of a typeface. It is typically conceived as the parent of a larger family.

Italic fonts, which are based on cursive writing, have forms distinct from roman.

ADOBE GARAMOND ITALIC

The italic form is not simply a mechanically slanted version of the roman: it is a separate typeface. Note that the letter a has a different shape in the roman and italic variants of Adobe Garamond.

SMALL CAPS HAVE A HEIGHT THAT IS SIMILAR TO *the lowercase* X-HEIGHT.

ADOBE GARAMOND EXPERT (SMALL CAPS)

Small caps (capitals) are designed to integrate with a line of text, where full-size capitals would stand out awkwardly. Small capitals are slightly taller than the x-height of lowercase letters.

Bold (and semibold) typefaces are used for emphasis within a hierarchy.

ADOBE GARAMOND BOLD AND SEMIBOLD

Bold versions of traditional text fonts were added in the twentieth century to meet the need for emphatic forms. Sans-serif families often include a broad range of weights (thin, bold, black, etc.).

Bold (and semibold) typefaces each need to include an italic version, too.

ADOBE GARAMOND BOLD AND SEMIBOLD ITALIC

The typeface designer tries to make the bold versions feel similar in contrast to the roman, without making the overall form too heavy. The counters need to stay clear and open at small sizes.

A full type family has two sets of numerals: *lining* (123) and *non-lining* (123).

ADOBE GARAMOND REGULAR AND EXPERT NUMERALS

Lining numerals occupy uniform units of horizontal space, so that the numbers line up when used in tabulated columns. Non-lining numerals, also called "text" or "old style" numerals, have a small body size plus ascenders and descenders, so that they mix well on a line with lowercase letters.

A *type* **family** CAN BE faked by *slanting,* or **inflating**, or SHRINKING letters.

ITALIC   BOLD   SMALL CAPS

TYPE CRIME:
PSEUDO ITALICS
The wide, ungainly forms of these skewed letters look forced and unnatural.

TYPE CRIME:
PSEUDO BOLD
Padded around the edges, these letters feel blunt and dull.

TYPE CRIME:
PSEUDO SMALL CAPS
These shrunken versions of full-size caps are puny and starved.

THESIS FAMILY

Designed by Lucas de Groot, LucasFonts, 1994
Thesis is one of the world's largest type families.

This is not a book about fonts. It is a book about how to use them. Typefaces
THESIS SERIF MEDIUM ROMAN

are essential resources for the graphic designer, just as glass, stone, steel, and
THESIS SERIF MEDIUM ITALIC

OTHER MATERIALS ARE EMPLOYED BY THE ARCHITECT. SOME DESIGNERS CREATE
THESIS SERIF MEDIUM SMALL CAPS

their own custom fonts. But most
THESIS SERIF BLACK ROMAN

regard to the audience or situation.
THESIS SERIF MEDIUM ROMAN

graphic designers will tap the vast
THESIS SERIF EXTRA BOLD ROMAN

Selecting type with wit and wisdom
THESIS SERIF SEMI LIGHT

store of already existing typefaces,
THESIS SERIF BOLD ROMAN

requires knowledge of how and why
THESIS SERIF LIGHT ROMAN

choosing and combining each with
THESIS SERIF SEMI BOLD ROMAN

letterforms have evolved. The history
THESIS SERIF EXTRA LIGHT ROMAN

of typography reflects a continual tension between the hand and machine, the
THESIS SANS MEDIUM ROMAN

organic and geometric, the human body and the abstract system. These tensions
THESIS SANS MEDIUM ITALIC

MARKED THE BIRTH OF PRINTED LETTERS FIVE CENTURIES AGO, AND THEY CONTINUE TO
THESIS SANS MEDIUM SMALL CAPS

energize typography today. Writing
THESIS SANS BLACK ROMAN

in Germany. Whereas documents and
THESIS SANS MEDIUM ROMAN

in the West was revolutionized early
THESIS SANS EXTRA BOLD ROMAN

books had previously been written by
THESIS SANS SEMI LIGHT ROMAN

in the Renaissance, when Johannes
THESIS SANS BOLD ROMAN

hand, printing with type mobilized all
THESIS SANS LIGHT ROMAN

Gutenberg introduced moveable type
THESIS SANS SEMI BOLD ROMAN

of the techniques of mass production.
THESIS SANS EXTRA LIGHT ROMAN

Interstate Light
Interstate Light Compressed
Interstate Light Condensed
Interstate Regular
Interstate Regular Compressed
Interstate Regular Condensed
Interstate Bold
Interstate Bold Compressed
Interstate Bold Condensed
Interstate Black
Interstate Black Compressed
Interstate Black Condensed

Designed by Tobias Frere-Jones, Font Bureau, 1993

UNIVERS *was designed by the Swiss typographer Adrian Frutiger in 1957. He designed 21 versions of Univers, in five weights and five widths. Whereas many typographic families grow over time as they become popular, Univers was conceived as a total system from its inception.*

Scala

Scala Italic

SCALA CAPS

Scala Bold

Scala Sans

Scala Sans Italic

SCALA SANS CAPS

Scala Sans Bold

Scala Sans Bold

SCALA JEWEL CRYSTAL

SCALA JEWEL DIAMOND

SCALA JEWEL PEARL

SCALA JEWEL SAPHYR

Martin Majoor's Scala, used throughout this book, began as a serif typeface. Majoor later added a sans-serif sub-family as well as an ornamental "jewel" set. Majoor's diagram above shows how the serif and sans-serif forms have a common spine.

A traditional roman book face typically has a small family—a "nuclear" group consisting of roman, italic, small caps, and possibly bold and semibold (each with an italic variant). Sans-serif families often come in many more weights and sizes, such as thin, light, black, compressed, and condensed. In the 1990s, many type designers created families that include both serif and sans-serif versions. Small capitals and non-lining numerals (a courtesy traditionally reserved for serif fonts) are included in the sans-serif versions of Thesis, Scala, and many other big contemporary families.

MERCURY BOLD SMALL CAPS
Proof, 2003
Designer: Jonathan Hoefler,
The Hoefler Type Foundry
*Mercury is designed for modern
newspaper production—fast, high-
volume printing on cheap paper.
The notes marked on this proof,
which shows sample letters from just
one variant of the vast Mercury
family, comment on everything from
the width or weight of a letter to the
size and shape of a serif.*

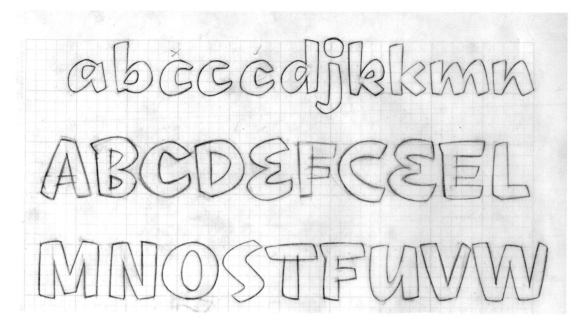

Castaways

LAS VEGAS: CASTAWAYS
Drawing and finished type, 2001
Art and type direction: Andy Cruz
Typeface design: Ken Barber
Font engineering: Rich Roat
House Industries

Castaways is from a series of digital fonts based on commercial signs in Las Vegas. The original signs were created by lettering artists who worked by hand to make custom graphics and logos. House Industries is a digital type foundry that creates typefaces inspired by popular culture and design history. Designer Ken Barber makes pencil drawings by hand and then digitizes the outlines.

For more than five hundred years, typeface production was an industrial process. Most type was cast from lead until the rise of photo typesetting in the 1960s and 1970s; early digital typefaces (also created in that period) still required specialized equipment for design and production. It was not until the introduction of desktop computers that typeface design became a widely accessible field. By the end of the twentieth century, digital "type foundries" had appeared around the globe, often run by one or two designers.

Producing a complete typeface remains, however, an enormous task. Even a relatively small type family has hundreds of distinct characters, each requiring many phases of refinement. The typeface designer must also determine how a font is to be spaced, what software platforms it will use, and how it will function in different sizes, media, and languages.

THE LOCUST (LEFT) AND
MELT BANANA (RIGHT)
Screenprint posters, 2002
Designer: Nolen Strals
Not all letters are typographic.
Hand lettering remains a
vibrant force in graphic design,
as seen in these posters
for Baltimore music events.
Hand lettering is also the basis
of many digital typefaces, but
there is nothing quite as potent
as the real thing.

Ingenieurbüro
Informations- und
Funktechnik

Johannes Hübner

Tel 0351-427 21 81
Fax 0351-427 21 91
Funk 0172-351 35 64

HÜBNER
Identity program, 1998
Designer: Jochen Stankowski
This identity for an engineering firm
uses the letter H *as a trademark.*
The proportions of the mark change
in different contexts.

Bünaustraße 21
01109 Dresden

Hübner

www.johannes-huebner.de
mail@johannes-huebner.de

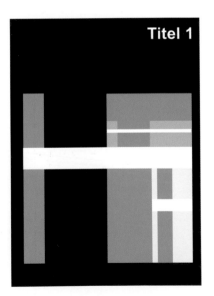

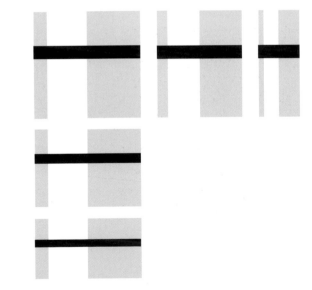

LOGOTYPES use typography or lettering to depict the name of an organization in a memorable way. Whereas some trademarks consist of an abstract symbol or a pictorial icon, a *logotype* uses letters to create a distinctive visual image.

　　Logotypes can be built with existing fonts or with custom-drawn letterforms. Modern logotypes are often designed in different versions for use in different situations. A logotype is part of an overall identity program, which the designer conceives as a "language" that lives (and changes) in various circumstances.

RACHEL COMEY
Logotypes, 2003
Designer: Anton Ginzburg
These logotypes for a fashion designer use traditional letterforms in a contemporary manner. Writing the designer's name in lowercase letters softens the formality of the classic script characters, while the capital letter M in "coMey" injects the name with an element of surprise.

THE NOGUCHI MUSEUM
Logotype, 2004
Designers: Abbott Miller and
Jeremy Hoffman, Pentagram
The sides of a square have been gently contoured in reference to the work of Isamu Noguchi, namesake of the Noguchi Museum. The concave square coordinates with the typeface Balance, used in the logotype, which also has softly curved elements.

LETTERSCAPES
Web site, 2002
Designer: Peter Cho
This experimental Web site
features bitmapped letters
animated in three-dimensional
space.

I became tired of cries for more *anti-aliased* type to correct the jagginess of digital type. While one side of me cried to see Garamond butchered on the pixel grid, another side thought, "Who cares?" John Maeda, 2001

Anti-aliasing, which uses shades of gray to create the illusion of a curved edge, is effective for presenting text on screen at large sizes.

At small sizes, however, anti-aliased text looks blurry. Many designers (and readers) prefer pixel fonts for text.

ANTI-ALIASED LETTER   BITMAPPED LETTER

Anti-aliasing creates the appearance of a smooth edge by rendering some of the pixels along the edge of the letter in shades of gray. It is more effective for displaying large headlines than small text.

FONTS FOR PRINT

Helvetica, created in Switzerland in 1957, is one of the most popular typefaces in the world.

Although Helvetica is the sans-serif default font for many computer users, it was designed for print.

12- AND 8-PT HELVETICA *Designed by Max Miedinger, 1957*

Times Roman, created for a London newspaper, is also hugely popular, owing largely to its broad distribution.

This font is a default for many Web sites, because users can be expected to have it on their own computers.

12- AND 8-PT TIMES *Designed by Stanley Morison, 1931*

FONTS FOR THE SCREEN

Verdana is a sans-serif font designed by Matthew Carter especially for digital display.

Verdana has a larger x-height, simpler curves, and more open forms than Helvetica.

12- AND 8-PT VERDANA *Designed by Matthew Carter, 1996*

Georgia is a serif screen face that is designed with simple curves, open forms, and generous letterspacing.

Georgia and Verdana, commissioned by Microsoft, have been widely distributed, making them useful Web fonts.

12- AND 8-PT GEORGIA *Designed by Matthew Carter, 1996*

Bitmap fonts are designed for digital display.

Bitmap fonts are designed for digital display at a specific size.

Bitmap fonts are designed for digital display.

Bitmap fonts are designed for digital display.

Bitmap fonts are designed for digital display at a specific size.

Bitmap fonts are designed for digital display at a specific size.

LO-RES FAMILY *Designed by Zuzana Licko for Emigre, 1985*
These bitmap fonts incorporate Licko's earlier Emigre, Emperor, Oakland, and Universal font families.

Bitmap fonts are designed for digital display at a specific size.
Bitmap fonts are designed for digital display at specific size.
Bitmap fonts are designed for digital display at specific size.
Bitmap fonts are designed for digital display at a specific size.

8-POT PIXELLA REGULAR, ITALIC, BOLD, AND BOLD ITALIC
Designed by Chester for Thirstype, 2003

Bitmap fonts are designed for digital display at a specific size.
Bitmap fonts are designed for digital display at a specific size.
Bitmap fonts are designed for digital display at a specific size.
Bitmap fonts are designed for digital display at a specific size.
Bitmap fonts are designed for digital display at a specific size.
Bitmap fonts are designed for digital display at a specific size.
Bitmap fonts are designed for digital display at a specific size.

8-PT FFF CORPORATE *Designed by Walter Apai for Fonts for Flash, 2003*
These fonts are designed specifically to work with the Macromedia Flash multimedia authoring application.

BITMAP FONTS are built out of the *pixels* (picture elements) that structure a screen display. Whereas a PostScript letter consists of a vectorized outline, a bitmap character contains a fixed number of rectilinear units that are either "on" or "off."

Outline fonts are *scalable*, meaning that they can be reproduced in a high-resolution medium such as print at nearly any size. Outline fonts are often hard to read on screen at small sizes, however, where all characters are translated into pixels. (Anti-aliasing can make legibility even worse for small text.) In a bitmap font, the pixels do not melt away as the letters get bigger. Some designers like to exploit this effect, which calls attention to the letters' digital geometry. Pixel fonts are widely used in both print and digital media.

8 px Corporate

16px Corporate

24px Corporate

32px Corporate

A bitmap font is designed to be used at a specific size, such as 8 pixels, because its body is precisely constructed out of screen units. A bitmap font should be displayed on screen in even multiples of its root size (enlarge 8-px type to 16, 24, 32, and so on).

```
BOEKHANDEL NIJHOF & LEE
   STAALSTRAAT 13-A
   1011 JK AMSTERDAM


22/05/03 13:12          01
000000 #0094    BED.1

VERZENDKOST.        42.50
TYPOGRAFIE           6.00
TYPOGRAFIE          16.50
TYPOGRAFIE          19.50
TYPOGRAFIE          33.95
TYPOGRAFIE          55.35
TYPOGRAFIE          32.00
TYPOGRAFIE          59.00
TYPOGRAFIE          40.00
TYPOGRAFIE          50.40
TYPOGRAFIE          47.25
TYPOGRAFIE          80.00
TYPOGRAFIE          37.70
SUBTOTAL           520.15
BTW LAAG            29.44

STUKS                 13Q
CREDIT          520.15

     DUK ANTIQUARIAAT
     TEL:020-6203980
     FAX:020-6393294
```

NIJHOF & LEE
Receipt, 2003
This cash register receipt, printed with a bitmap font, is from a design and typography bookstore in Amsterdam. (The author is still in debt from this transaction.)

Create a prototype for a bitmap font by designing letters on a grid of squares. Substitute the curves and diagonals of traditional letterforms with rectilinear elements. Avoid making detailed "staircases," which are just curves and diagonals in disguise. This exercise looks back to the 1910s and 1920s, when avant-garde designers made experimental typefaces out of simple geometric parts. The project also reflects the structure of digital technologies, from cash register receipts and LED signs to on-screen font display, showing how a typeface functions as a system of elements.

Examples of student work from Maryland Institute College of Art

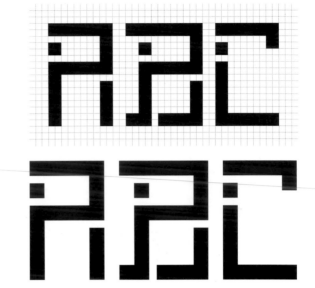

WENDY NEESE

JAMES ALVAREZ

JOEY POTTS

BRUCE WILLEN

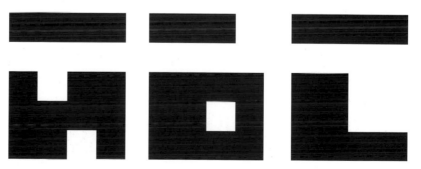

BRENDON MCCLEAN

THE XIX AMENDMENT
Typographic installation in Grand Central Station,
New York City, 1995
Designer: Stephen Doyle
Client: The New York State Division of Women
Sponsors: The New York State Division of Women,
the Metropolitan Transportation Authority, Revlon,
and Merrill Lynch

TEXT

CYBERSPACE AND CIVIL
SOCIETY
Poster, 1996
Designer: Hayes Henderson
*Rather than represent
cyberspace as an ethereal grid,
the designer has used blotches
of overlapping text to build an
ominous, looming body.*

TEXT

LETTERS GATHER INTO WORDS, WORDS BUILD INTO SENTENCES.
In typography, "text" is defined as an ongoing sequence of words, distinct
from shorter headlines or captions. The main block is often called the
"body," comprising the principal mass of content. Also known as "running
text," it can flow from one page, column, or box to another. Text can be
viewed as a thing—a sound and sturdy object—or a fluid poured into the
containers of page or screen. Text can be solid or liquid, body or blood.

As body, text has more integrity and wholeness than the elements
that surround it, from pictures, captions, and page numbers to banners,
buttons, and menus. Designers generally treat a body of text consistently,
letting it appear as a coherent substance that is distributed across the spaces
of a document. In digital media, long texts are typically broken into chunks
that can be accessed by search engines or hypertext links. Contemporary
designers and writers produce content for various contexts, from the pages
of print to an array of software environments, screen conditions, and digital
devices, each posing its own limits and opportunities.

Designers provide ways into—and out of—the flood of words
by breaking up text into pieces and offering shortcuts and alternate routes
through masses of information. From a simple indent (signaling the
entrance to a new idea) to a highlighted link (announcing a jump to another
location), typography helps readers navigate the flow of content. The user
could be searching for a specific piece of data or struggling to quickly
process a volume of content in order to extract elements for immediate use.
Although many books define the purpose of typography as enhancing the
readability of the written word, one of design's most humane functions is,
in actuality, to help readers *avoid* reading.

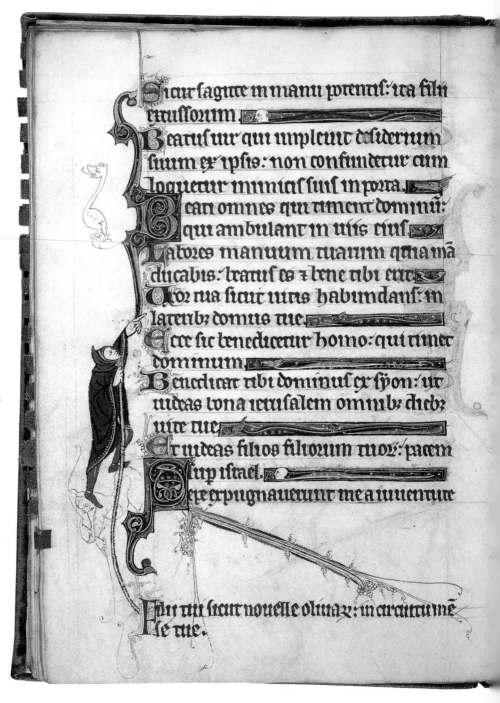

ERRORS AND OWNERSHIP

Typography helped seal the literary notion of "the text" as a complete, original work, a stable body of ideas expressed in an essential form. Before the invention of printing, handwritten documents were riddled with errors. Copies were copied from copies, each with its own glitches and gaps. Scribes devised inventive ways to insert missing lines into manuscripts in order to salvage and repair these laboriously crafted objects.

Printing with movable type was the first system of mass production, replacing the hand-copied manuscript. As in other forms of mass production, the cost of setting type, insuring its correctness, and running a press drops for each unit as the size of the print run increases. Labor and capital are invested in tooling and preparing the technology, rather than in making the individual unit. The printing system allows editors and authors to correct a work as it passes from handwritten manuscript to typographic galley. "Proofs" are test copies made before final production begins. The proofreader's craft ensures the faithfulness of the printed text to the author's handwritten original.

Yet even the text that has passed through the castle gates of print is inconstant. Each edition of a book represents one fossil record of a text, a record that changes every time the work is translated, quoted, revised, interpreted, or taught. Since the rise of digital tools for writing and publishing, manuscript originals have all but vanished. ~~Electronic redlining is replacing the hieroglyphics of the editor.~~ On-line texts can be downloaded by users and reformatted, repurposed, and recombined.

Print helped establish the figure of the author as the owner of a text, and copyright laws were written in the early eighteenth century to protect the author's rights to this property. The digital age is riven by battles between those who argue, on the one hand, for the fundamental liberty of data and ideas, and those who hope to protect—sometimes indefinitely—the investment made in publishing and authoring content.

A classic typographic page emphasizes the completeness and closure of a work, its authority as a finished product. Alternative design strategies in the twentieth and twenty-first centuries reflect the contested nature of authorship by revealing the openness of texts to the flow of information and the corrosiveness of history.

Marshall McLuhan, *The Gutenberg Galaxy* (Toronto: University of Toronto Press, 1962).

On the future of intellectual property, see Lawrence Lessig, *Free Culture: How Big Media Uses Technology and the Law to Lock Down Culture and Control Creativity* (New York: Penguin, 2004).

Typography tended to alter language from a means of perception and exploration to a portable commodity. Marshall McLuhan, 1962

THE TELEPHONE BOOK:
TECHNOLOGY, SCHIZO-
PHRENIA, ELECTRIC SPEECH
Book, 1989
Designer: Richard Eckersley
Author: Avital Ronell
Compositor: Michael Jensen
Publisher: University of
Nebraska Press
Photograph: Dan Meyers
This book, a philosophical study of writing as a material technology, uses typography to emphasize the rhetorical argument of the text. This spread, for example, is fractured by typographic "rivers," spaces that connect vertically through the page. Rivers violate the even, unified texture that is a sacred goal within traditional typographic design.

"How indeed could I aim my argument at some singular destination, at one or another among you whose proper name I might for example know? And then, is knowing a proper name tantamount to knowing someone?" (*MC*, 2). Derrida demonstrates for his part that the most general structure of the mark participates in a speech destined in advance to addressees (*destinataires*) who are not easily determinable or who, as far as any possible calculation is concerned, in any case command a great reserve of indetermination. This involves a language operating as a system of marks: "Language, however, is only one among those systems of *marks* that claim this curious tendency as their property: they *simultaneously* incline towards increasing the reserves of random indetermination *as well as* the capacity for coding and overcoding or, in other words, for control and self-regulation" (*MC*, 2). We begin to discern how the simultaneity of determining, coding, and even supercoding forms a deep cooperation with the inclination in language toward anticoding, or what Derrida sees as the inflated reserves of random indeterminateness. This double-edged coding, we must remember, regards, as it were, nonschizophrenic language, if such a thing there be. "Such competition between randomness and code disrupts the very systematicity of the system while it also, however, regulates the restless, unstable interplay of the system. Whatever its singularity in this respect, the linguistic system of these traces or marks would merely be, it seems to me, just a particular example of the law of destabilization" (*MC*, 2). It may be useful to note that Derrida understands language in terms primarily of traces and marks, where Lainguage concerns signs in the first place, and in particular the broken rapport of that which is signifying to what ostensibly lies hidden behind it, or the disconnection between signs and signs or signs and referents. Laing is led to assume the latency of a single, unique, localizable but timid presence—rather than trace or residual mark—from where it could be securely determined who speaks, and to whom. This all too brief excursion into "My Chances," which may unwittingly reproduce the effect and trauma of a chance encounter, means to engage a dialogue between the question of address raised by Laing and the ones raised in turn by Derrida. For it now appears that Laing places his bets on the sustained systematicity of the system which Derrida shows always already to fall under a law of destabilization.[89] Moreover, Derrida does not suggest lan-

SPACING

Design is as much an act of spacing as an act of marking. The typographer's art concerns not only the positive grain of letterforms, but the negative gaps between and around them. In letterpress printing, every space is constructed by a physical object, a blank piece of metal or wood with no raised image. The faceless slugs of lead and slivers of copper inserted as spaces between words or letters are as physical as the relief characters around them. Thin strips of lead (called "leading") divide the horizontal lines of type; wider blocks of "furniture" hold the margins of the page.

Although we take the breaks between words for granted, spoken language is perceived as a continuous flow, with no audible gaps. Spacing has become crucial, however, to alphabetic writing, which translates the sounds of speech into multiple characters. Spaces were introduced after the invention of the Greek alphabet to make words intelligible as distinct units. Tryreadingalineoftextwithoutspacingtoseehowimportantithasbecome.

With the invention of typography, spacing and punctuation ossified from gap and gesture to physical artifact. Punctuation marks, which were used differently from one scribe to another in the manuscript era, became part of the standardized, rule-bound apparatus of the printed page. The communications scholar Walter Ong has shown how printing converted the word into a visual object precisely located in space: "Alphabet letterpress printing, in which each letter was cast on a separate piece of metal, or type, marked a psychological breakthrough of the first order....Print situates words in space more relentlessly than writing ever did. Writing moves words from the sound world to the world of visual space, but print locks words into position in this space." Typography made text into a thing, a material object with known dimensions and fixed locations.

Walter Ong, *Orality and Literacy: The Technologizing of the Word* (London and New York: Methuen, 1981). See also Jacques Derrida, *Of Grammatology*, trans. Gayatri Chakravorty Spivak (Baltimore: Johns Hopkins University Press, 1976).

The French philosopher Jacques Derrida, who devised the theory of deconstruction in the 1960s, wrote that although the alphabet represents sound, it cannot function without silent marks and spaces. Typography manipulates the silent dimensions of the alphabet, employing habits and techniques—such as spacing and punctuation—that are seen but not heard. The alphabet, rather than evolve into a transparent code for recording speech, developed its own visual resources, becoming a more powerful technology as it left behind its connections to the spoken word.

That a speech supposedly alive can lend itself to spacing in its own writing is what relates to its own death. Jacques Derrida, 1976

LINEARITY

In his essay "From Work to Text," the French critic Roland Barthes presented two opposing models of writing: the closed, fixed "work" versus the open, unstable "text." In Barthes's view, the work is a tidy, neatly packaged object, proofread and copyrighted, made perfect and complete by the art of printing. The text, in contrast, is impossible to contain, operating across a dispersed web of standard plots and received ideas. Barthes pictured the text as "woven entirely with citations, references, echoes, cultural languages (what language is not?), antecedent and contemporary, which cut across and through in a vast stereophony....The metaphor of the Text is that of the *network*." Writing in the 1960s and 1970s, Barthes anticipated the Internet as a decentralized web of connections.

Roland Barthes, "From Work to Text," *Image/Music/Text,* trans. Stephen Heath (New York: Hill and Wang, 1977), 155–64.

Barthes was describing literature, yet his ideas resonate for typography, the visual manifestation of language. The singular "body" of the traditional text page has long been supported by the navigational features of the book, from page numbers and headings that mark a reader's location to such tools as the index, appendix, abstract, footnote, and table of contents. These devices were able to emerge because the typographic book is a fixed sequence of pages, a body lodged in a grid of known coordinates.

All such devices are attacks on linearity, providing means of entrance and escape from the one-way stream of discourse. Whereas talking flows in a single direction, writing occupies space as well as time. Tapping that spatial dimension—and thus liberating readers from the bonds of linearity—is among typography's most urgent tasks.

Although digital media are commonly celebrated for their potential as nonlinear potential communication, linearity nonetheless thrives in the electronic realm, from the "CNN crawl" that marches along the bottom of the television screen to the ticker-style LED signs that loop through the urban environment. Film titles—the celebrated convergence of typography and cinema—serve to distract the audience from the inescapable tedium of a contractually decreed, top-down disclosure of ownership and authorship.

Linearity dominates many of the commercial software applications that have claimed to revolutionize everyday writing and communication. Word processing programs, for example, treat documents as a linear stream. (In contrast, page layout programs such as Quark XPress and Adobe InDesign allow users to work spatially, breaking up text into columns and

A text...is a multi-dimensional space in which a variety of writings, none of them original, blend and clash. Roland Barthes, 1971

On the linearity of word processing, see Nancy Kaplan, "Blake's Problem and Ours: Some Reflections on the Image and the Word," *Readerly/Writerly Texts*, 3.2 (Spring/Summer 1996), 125. On PowerPoint, see Edward R. Tufte, "The Cognitive Style of PowerPoint," (Cheshire, Conn.: Graphics Press, 2003).

pages that can be anchored and landmarked.) PowerPoint and other presentation software programs are supposed to illuminate the spoken word by guiding the audience through the linear unfolding of an oral address. Typically, however, PowerPoint enforces the one-way flow of speech rather than alleviating it. While a single sheet of paper could provide a map or summary of an oral presentation, a PowerPoint show drags out in time across numerous screens.

Not all digital media favor linear flow over spatial arrangement, however. The database, one of the defining information structures of our time, is an essentially nonlinear form. Providing readers and writers with a simultaneous menu of options, a database is a system of elements that can be arranged in countless sequences. Page layouts are built on the fly from freestanding chunks of information, assembled in response to user feedback. The Web is pushing authors, editors, and designers to work inventively with new modes of "microcontent" (page titles, key words, alt tags) that allow data to be searched, indexed, bookmarked, translated into audio, or otherwise marked for recall.

On the aethetics of the database, see Lev Manovich, *The Language of New Media* (Cambridge: MIT Press, 2002).

Databases are the structure behind electronic games, magazines, and catalogues, genres that create an information *space* rather than a linear *sequence*. Physical stores and libraries are databases of tangible objects found in the built environment. Media critic Lev Manovich has described language itself as a kind of database, an archive of elements from which people assemble the linear utterances of speech. Many design projects call for the emphasis of space over sequence, system over utterance, simultaneous structure over linear narrative. Contemporary design often combines aspects of architecture, typography, film, wayfinding, branding, and other modes of address. By dramatizing the spatial quality of a project, designers can foster understanding of complex documents or environments.

The history of typography is marked by the increasingly sophisticated use of space. In the digital age, where characters are accessed by keystroke and mouse, not gathered from heavy drawers of manufactured units, space has become more liquid than concrete, and typography has evolved from a stable body of objects to a flexible system of attributes.

Database and narrative are natural enemies. Competing for the same territory of human culture, each claims an exclusive right to make meaning of the world. Lev Manovich, 2002

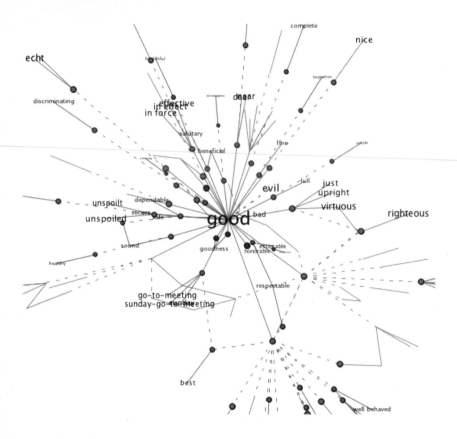

echt

complete

nice

helpful

discriminating

effective
in force
irrupt

dear

salutary

superior

beneficial

fine

simple

evil

full

just
upright

unspoilt

dependable

secure

safe

virtuous

righteous

unspoiled

good

bad

sound

goodness

estimable
honorable

healthy

respectable

go-to-meeting
sunday-go-to-meeting

best

well-behaved

VISUAL THESAURUS 2.0
Interactive media, 2003
Designers: Plumb Design Inc.
This digital thesaurus presents words within a three-dimensional
web of relationships. The central term is linked to nodes representing
that word's different senses. The more connections each of these
satellite nodes contains, the bigger and closer it appears on the
screen. Clicking on a satellite word brings that term to the center.

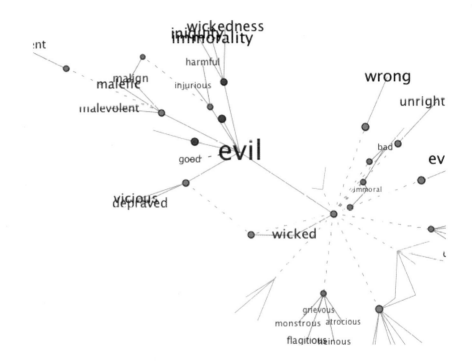

Succeeding the Author, the scriptor no longer bears within him passions, humours, feelings, impressions, but rather this immense dictionary from which he draws a writing that can know no halt. Roland Barthes, 1968

KATHERINE McCoy
MICHAEL McCoy

ART science

Nothing pulls you into the territory between art and science quite so quickly as design. It is the borderline where contradictions and tensions exist between the quantifiable and the poetic. It is the field between desire and necessity. Designers thrive in those conditions, moving between land and water. A typical critique at Cranbrook can easily move in a matter of minutes between

MATHEMATIC poetic

a discussion of the object as a validation of being to the precise mechanical proposal for actuating the object. The discussion moves from Heidegger to the "strange material of the week" or from Lyotard to printing technologies without missing a beat. The free flow of ideas, and the leaps from the technical to the mythical, stem from the attempt to maintain a studio plat-

DESIRE necessity

find his or her own voice as a designer. The form that supports each student's search to **the** **new** and faculty to encounter their own studio is a hothouse that enables students process that is at times chaotic, visions of the world and act on them — a conflicting, and occasionally inspiring.

Watching the process of students absorbing new ideas and influences, and the incredible range of interpretations of those ideas into design, is

MYTHOLOGY technology

an annual experience that is always amazing. In recent years, for example, the de- **discourse** partment has had the experience of watching wood craftsmen metamorphose into high technologists, and graphic designers into software humanists. Yet it all seems consistent. They are bringing a very personal vision to an area that desperately needs it. The messiness of human experi-

PURIST pluralist

ence is warming up the cold precision of technology to make it livable, and lived in.

Unlike the Bauhaus, Cranbrook never embraced a singular teaching method or philosophy, other than Saarinen's exhortation to each student to find his or her own way, in the company of other artists and designers who were engaged in the same search. The energy at Cranbrook seems to come from the fact of

INDIVIDUAL communal

the mutual search, although not the mutual conclusion. If design is about life, why shouldn't it have all the complexity, variety, contradiction, and sublimity of life?

Much of the work done at **Cranbrook** has been dedicated to changing the status quo. It is polemical, calculated to ruffle designers' feathers. And

DANGEROUS rigorous

BIRTH OF THE USER

Roland Barthes's model of the text as an open web of references, rather than a closed and perfect work, asserts the importance of the reader over the writer in creating meaning. The reader "plays" the text as a musician plays an instrument. The author does not control its significance: "the text itself plays (like a door, like a machine with 'play') and the reader plays twice over, playing the Text as one plays a game, looking for a practice that reproduces it" (102). Like an interpretation of a musical score, reading is a performance of the written word.

Graphic designers embraced the idea of the readerly text in the 1980s and early 1990s, using layers of text and interlocking grids to explore Barthes's theory of the "death of the author." In place of the classical model of typography as a crystal goblet for content, this alternative view assumes that content itself changes with each act of representation. Typography becomes a mode of interpretation.

Redefining typography as "discourse," designer Katherine McCoy imploded the traditional dichotomy between seeing and reading. Pictures can be read (analyzed, decoded, taken apart), and words can be seen (perceived as icons, forms, patterns). Valuing ambiguity and complexity, her approach challenged readers to produce their own meanings while trying also to elevate the status of designers within the process of authorship.

Another model, which undermined the designer's new claim to power, surfaced at the end of the 1990s, borrowed not from literary criticism but from human-computer interaction (HCI) studies and the fields of interface and usability design. The dominant subject of our age has become neither reader nor writer but *user*, a figure conceived as a bundle of needs and impairments—cognitive, physical, emotional. Like a patient or child, the user is a figure to be protected and cared for but also scrutinized and controlled, submitted to research and testing.

How texts are *used* becomes more important than what they mean. Someone clicked here to get over there. Someone who bought this also bought that. The interactive environment not only provides users with a degree of control and self-direction but also, more quietly and insidiously, it gathers data about its audiences. Barthes's image of the text as a game to be played still holds, as the user respond to signals from the system. We may play the text, but it is also playing us.

CRANBROOK DESIGN:
THE NEW DISCOURSE
Book, 1990
Designers:
Katherine McCoy,
P. Scott Makela, and
Mary Lou Kroh
Publisher: Rizzoli
Photograph: Dan Meyers
Under the direction of Katherine and Michael McCoy, the graduate program in graphic and industrial design at Cranbrook Academy of Art was a leading center for experimental design from the 1970s through the early 1990s. Katherine McCoy developed a model of "typography as discourse," in which the designer and reader actively interpret an author's text.

Design a human-machine interface in accordance with the abilities and foibles of humankind, and you will help the user not only get the job done, but be a happier, more productive person.
Jef Raskin, 2000

Graphic designers can use theories of user interaction to revisit some of our basic assumptions about visual communication. Why, for example, are readers on the Web less patient than readers of print? It is commonly believed that digital displays are inherently more difficult to read than ink on paper. Yet HCI studies conducted in the late 1980s proved that crisp black text on a white background can be read just as efficiently from a screen as from a printed page.

The impatience of the digital reader arises from culture, not from the essential character of display technologies. Users of Web sites have different expectations than users of print. They expect to feel "productive," not contemplative. They expect to be in search mode, not processing mode. Users also expect to be disappointed, distracted, and delayed by false leads. The cultural habits of the screen are driving changes in design for print, while at the same time affirming print's role as a place where extended reading can still occur.

Another common assumption is that icons are a more universal mode of communication than text. Icons are central to the GUIs (graphical user interfaces) that routinely connect users with computers. Yet text can often provide a more specific and understandable cue than a picture. Icons don't actually simplify the translation of content into multiple languages, because they require explanation in multiple languages. The endless icons of the digital desktop, often rendered with gratuitous detail and depth, function more to enforce brand identity than to support usability. In the twentieth century, modern designers hailed pictures as a "universal" language, yet in the age of code, text has become a more common denominator than images—searchable, translatable, and capable of being reformatted and restyled for alternative or future media.

Perhaps the most persistent impulse of twentieth-century art and design was to physically integrate form and content. The Dada and Futurist poets, for example, used typography to create texts whose content was inextricable from the concrete layout of specific letterforms on a page. In the twenty-first century, form and content are being pulled back apart. Style sheets, for example, compel designers to think globally and systematically instead of focusing on the fixed construction of a particular surface. This way

On screen readability, see John D. Gould *et al.*, "Reading from CRT Displays Can Be as Fast as Reading from Paper," *Human Factors*, 29, 5 (1987): 497–517.

On the restless user, see Jakob Nielsen, *Designing Web Usability* (Indianapolis: New Riders, 2000).

On the failure of interface icons, see Jef Raskin, *The Humane Interface: New Directions for Designing Interactive Systems* (Reading, Mass.: Addison-Wesley, 2000).

Web users don't like to read....They want to keep moving and clicking.
Jakob Nielsen, 2000

of thinking allows content to be reformatted for different devices or users, and it also prepares for the afterlife of data as electronic storage media begin their own cycles of decay and obsolescence.

In the twentieth century, modern artists and critics asserted that each medium is specific. They defined film, for example, as a constructive language distinct from theater, and they described painting as a physical medium that refers to its own processes. Today, however, the medium is not always the message. Design has become a "transmedia" enterprise, as authors and producers create worlds of characters, places, situations, and interactions that can appear across a variety of products. A game might live in different versions on a video screen, a desktop computer, a game console, and a cell phone, as well as on t-shirts, lunch boxes, and plastic toys.

The beauty and wonder of "white space" is another modernist myth that is subject to revision in the age of the user. Modern designers discovered that open space on a page can have as much physical presence as printed areas. White space is not always a mental kindness, however. Edward Tufte, a fierce advocate of visual density, argues for maximizing the amount of data conveyed on a single page or screen. In order to help readers make connections and comparisons as well as to find information quickly, a single surface packed with well-organized information is sometimes better than multiple pages with a lot of blank space. In typography as in urban life, density invites intimate exchange among people and ideas.

In our much-fabled era of information overload, a person can still process only one message at a time. This brute fact of cognition is the secret behind magic tricks: sleights of hand occur while the attention of the audience is drawn elsewhere. Given the fierce competition for their attention, users have a chance to shape the information economy by choosing what to look at. Designers can help them make satisfying choices.

Typography is an interface to the alphabet. User theory tends to favor normative solutions over innovative ones, pushing design into the background. Readers usually ignore the typographic interface, gliding comfortably along literacy's habitual groove. Sometimes, however, the interface should be allowed to fail. By making itself evident, typography can illuminate the construction and identity of a page, screen, place, or product.

On transmedia design thinking, see Brenda Laurel, *Utopian Entrepreneur* (Cambridge: MIT Press, 2001).

Jef Raskin talks about the scarcity of human attention as well as the myth of white space in *The Humane Interface: New Directions for Designing Interactive Systems*, cited on p. 74.

If people weren't good at finding tiny things in long lists, the *Wall Street Journal* would have gone out of business years ago. Jef Raskin, 2000

TYPOGRAPHY, INVENTED IN THE RENAISSANCE, allowed text to become a fixed and stable form. Like the body of the letter, the body of text was transformed by print into an industrial commodity that gradually became more open and flexible.

Critics of electronic media have noted that the rise of networked communication did not lead to the much feared destruction of typography (or even to the death of print), but rather to the burgeoning of the alphabetic empire. As Peter Lunenfeld points out, the computer has revived the power and prevalence of writing: "Alphanumeric text has risen from its own ashes, a digital phoenix taking flight on monitors, across networks, and in the realms of virtual space." The computer display is more hospitable to text than the screens of film or television because it offers physical proximity, user control, and a scale appropriate to the body.

The book is no longer the chief custodian of the written word. Branding is a powerful variant of literacy that revolves around symbols, icons, and typographic standards, leaving its marks on buildings, packages, album covers, Web sites, store displays, and countless other surfaces and spaces. With the expansion of the Internet, new (and old) conventions for displaying text quickly congealed, adapting metaphors from print and architecture: window, frame, page, banner, menu. Designers working within this stream of multiple media confront text in myriad forms, giving shape to extended bodies but also to headlines, decks, captions, notes, pull quotes, logotypes, navigation bars, alt tags, and other prosthetic clumps of language that announce, support, and even eclipse the main body of text.

The dissolution of writing is most extreme in the realm of the Web, where distracted readers safeguard their time and prize function over form. This debt of restlessness is owed not to the essential nature of computer monitors, but to the new behaviors engendered by the Internet, a place of searching and finding, scanning and mining. The reader, having toppled the author's seat of power during the twentieth century, now ails and lags, replaced by the dominant subject of our own era: the *user*, a figure whose scant attention is our most coveted commodity. Do not squander it.

On electronic writing, see Peter Lunenfeld, *Snap to Grid: A User's Guide to Digital Arts, Media, and Cultures* (Cambridge: MIT Press, 2001); Jay David Bolter, *Writing Space: Computers, Hypertext, and the Remediation of Print* (Mahwah, NJ: Lawrence Erlbaum Associates, 2001), and Stuart Moulthrop, "You Say You Want a Revolution? Hypertext and the Laws of Media," *The New Media Reader*, ed. Noah Wardrip-Fruin and Nick Monfort (Cambridge: MIT Press, 2003), 691–703.

Hypertext means the end of the death of literature. Stuart Moulthrop, 1991

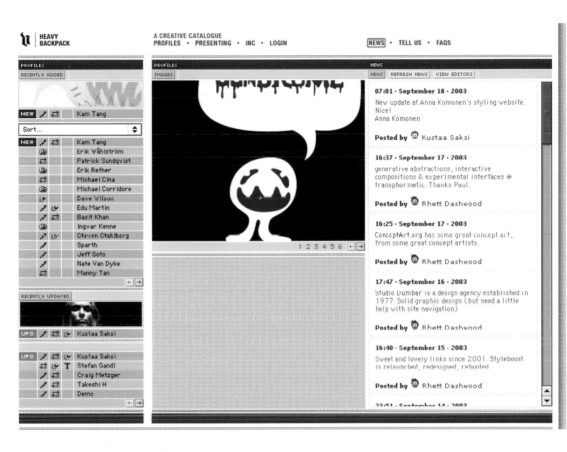

HEAVY BACKPACK
Web site, 2003
*A celebration of visual density
is seen in this site that collects
and annotates links to other
sites.*

The corpse of the Australopithecus he had
killed lay nude before him. Using two flat
stones, he made a cradle to hold his music,
the thick book of mysteries he had found
in the weeds: *Grant's Anatomy and Dissector*.
He knelt down beside her, a cellist about to
perform. *Hold the scalpel like a cello bow,*
he read, gripping a sharpened clam shell.
Then—a quick check against the diagram
in the book—he pressed the shell's point
into the ape-woman's chest   he flesh yielded
easily, blood oozing out not as from a mortal
puncture but with no pressure or urgency,
as though it was okay, and he continued his
bow's stroke—the low opening of a requiem—
gaining confidence as he lengthened the
incision toward her *Mons Veneris* (*fig. A*).
He wiped the sweat from his eyes. Since she
was more simian than a Neanderthal, he had
expected her hide to be at least as thick as
a callus so was surprised to find how much
like himself an Australopithecus could be.

Do we not have hands,
organs, dimensions?...

ppp

He took a deep breath, then began a second
long cut, curving around the other breast,
then the navel, duplicating the pattern
in the book till her torso was dominated
by a brilliant red **Y**
...senses, affections, passions?—

As it said in *Grant's*, Square cut a "buttonhole"
near her navel. Hooking a finger through it Are we not fed with the
he pulled the skin of her torso up and over her same food, hurt with the
face. Just as quick, she was transfigured before same weapons, subject to
him: a shimmering anatomical sculpture of ropy the same diseases?...
muscles, pink and red with striations of yellow fat.
A scent of fresh meat wafted up, making his
nostrils twitch.

In the book, transparent overlays, smooth
as membranes, presented the body as layers
where everything rhymed, and turning a leaf,
he wished it were that easy. His thumb left
a bloody smudge print on one stanza.
...*divide the pleura, being careful to*....

U.S. PATENT No. **5506131**
TRANSGENIC ANIMAL MODELS OF INFLAMMATORY DISEASE

r« **B** »c

VAS: AN OPERA IN FLATLAND
Book, 2002
Designer: Stephen Farrell
Author: Steve Tomasula
Publisher: Station Hill Press,
*In this typographic novel about
post-genetic civilization, texts
and images align against a
series of thin rules incising the
outer margins. The boldface
letters along the flush edge of
the text body accentuate the
column structure. The book is
printed throughout in three
colors (flesh, blood, and black).
The body of text is explored as
an open system.*

Takes two

SCALA, WITH KERNING SUPPRESSED
Spacing appears uneven, with gaps around the T and w.

Takes two

SCALA, WITH KERNING
Spacing seems more even, although some characters nearly touch.

nearly touch

SCALA ITALIC, WITH KERNING SUPPRESSED
A gap appears between the l and y.

nearly touch

SCALA ITALIC, WITH KERNING
The characteristic intimacy of italic requires kerning.

KERNING If letters in a typeface are spaced too uniformly, they make a pattern that doesn't look uniform enough. Gaps occur, for example, around letters whose forms angle outward or frame an open space (W, Y, V, T, L). In metal type, a *kerned* letter extends past the lead slug that supports it, allowing two letters to sit more closely together. In the digital typefaces used today, the space between letters is controlled by a table of *kerning pairs*, which specify spaces between different letter combinations.

LOVE LETTERS

The VE and TT combinations make the words look mismatched.

LOVE LETTERS

Kerning has been manually adjusted for a more even appearance.

rub my back

rub my back

KERNING LARGER SIZES Because the space between characters expands as the type size increases, designers often fine-tune letterspacing when working with large letters. As the word "rub" gets bigger, the gap between *u* and *b* grows more obvious.

rub my back

TYPE CRIME:
TOO MUCH SPACE
Mind the gap,
especially at larger sizes.

TRACKING Adjusting the overall space between letters, rather than the space between two characters, is called *tracking*, also known as letterspacing. It is common practice to letterspace capitals and small capitals, which appear more regal when standing apart. By slightly expanding the tracking across a body of text, the designer can create a more airy field. Negative tracking is rarely desirable. This device should be used sparingly, to adjust one or more lines of justified type.

Lowercase letters respond less favorably to letterspacing than do uppercase letters, because they are designed to sit together intimately on a line.

LOVE LETTERS
SCALA CAPITALS, NORMAL TRACKING

LOVE LETTERS
SCALA CAPITALS, LOOSE TRACKING

LOVE LETTERS   LOVE LETTERS
SCALA SMALL CAPITALS, NORMAL VS. LOOSE TRACKING

love letters *love letters*
SCALA, ROMAN AND ITALIC, LOOSE TRACKING

love letters *love letters*
SCALA, ROMAN AND ITALIC, NORMAL TRACKING

NORMAL TRACKING
Letters do love one another. However, due to their anatomical differences, some letters have a hard time achieving intimacy. Consider the letter *V*, for example, whose seductive valley makes her limbs stretch out above her base. In contrast, *L* solidly holds his ground yet harbors a certain emptiness above the waist. Automated kerning tables solve these problems in most situations, but some letters may require personal attention at larger sizes. Capital letters, being square and conservative, prefer to keep a little distance from their neighbors.

POSITIVE TRACKING
Letters do love one another. However, due to their anatomical differences, some letters have a hard time achieving intimacy. Consider the letter *V*, for example, whose seductive valley makes her limbs stretch out above her base. In contrast, *L* who solidly holds his ground yet harbors a certain emptiness above the waist. Automated kerning tables solve these problems in most situations, but some letters may require personal attention at larger sizes. Capital letters, being square and conservative, prefer to keep a little distance from their neighbors.

NEGATIVE TRACKING
Letters do love one another. However, due to their anatomical differences, some letters have a hard time achieving intimacy. Consider the letter *V*, for example, whose seductive valley makes her limbs stretch out above her base. In contrast, *L* solidly holds his ground yet harbors a certain emptiness above the waist. Automated kerning tables solve these problems in most situations, but some letters may require additional guidance at larger sizes. Capital letters, being square and conservative, prefer to keep a little distance from their neighbors.

TYPE CRIME:
NEGATIVE TRACKING
Make the shoe fit, not the foot. Don't use negative tracking to save space.

Ancient maps of the world

An

when the world was flat

Avid

inform us, concerning the void

Dream

where America was waiting

Of

to be discovered,

Trans-

Here Be Dragons. James Baldwin

for-

O to be a dragon. Marianne Moore

mation

Adrienne Kennedy, *People Who Led to My Plays*

MARGO JEFFERSON

DANCE INK: AN AVID DREAM
OF TRANSFORMATION
Magazine page, 1992
Designer: Abbott Miller
Publisher: Patsy Tarr
The extreme line spacing
(leading) allows two strands
of text to interweave.

The distance from the baseline of one line of type to another is called *line spacing*. It is also called *leading*, in reference to the strips of lead used to separate lines of metal type. The default setting in most layout and imaging software is slightly greater than the cap height of the letters. Expanding this distance creates a text block with a lighter, more open color. As line spacing increases further, the lines of type become independent linear elements rather than parts of an overall texture.

The distance from the baseline of one line of type to another is called *line spacing*. It is also called *leading*, in reference to the strips of lead used to separate lines of metal type. The default setting in most layout and imaging software is slightly greater than the cap height of the letters. Expanding this distance creates a text block with a lighter, more open color. As line spacing increases further, the lines of type become independent linear elements rather than parts of an overall texture.

The distance from the baseline of one line of type to another is called *line spacing*. It is also called *leading*, in reference to the strips of lead used to separate lines of metal type. The default setting in most layout and imaging software is slightly greater than the cap height of the letters. Expanding this distance creates a text block with a lighter, more open color. As line spacing increases further, the lines of type become independent linear elements rather than parts of an overall texture.

The distance from the baseline of one line of type to another is called *line spacing*. It is also called *leading*, in reference to the strips of lead used to separate lines of metal type. The default setting in most layout and imaging software is slightly greater than the cap height of the letters. Expanding this distance creates a text block with a lighter, more open color. As line spacing increases further, the lines of type become independent linear elements rather than parts of an overall texture.

7/7 SCALA
7-pt type with
7 pts line spacing

This is called "set solid." When lines are set this closely together, the ascenders and descenders begin to touch, an uncomfortable effect.

7/8.5 SCALA
Auto spacing; 7-pt type with
8.5 pts line spacing

In most page layout programs, the default line spacing (leading) is 120%, or slightly greater than the cap height.

7/9 SCALA
7-pt type with
9 pts line spacing

This column is set with wider line spacing (leading) than the standard default.

7/10 SCALA
7-pt type with
10 pts line spacing

As the line spacing becomes more extreme, the block of text begins to read as separate lines rather than a shade of gray.

The arrangement of text into columns with hard or soft edges is called *alignment*. Each basic style of alignment brings aesthetic qualities and potential hazards to the design of page or screen. *Justified* text, which has even edges on both left and right, has been the norm since the invention of printing with movable type, which enabled the creation of page after page of straight-edged columns. Justified type makes efficient use of space, and it also creates a clean shape on the page. Ugly gaps can occur, however, when the line length is too short in relation to the size of type used. Hyphenation breaks up long words and helps keep the lines of text tightly packed. Letterspacing can also be used to to adjust a line.

In *flush left/ragged right* text, the left edge is hard and the right edge is soft. Word spaces do not fluctuate, so there are never big holes inside the lines of text. This format, which was rarely used before the twentieth century, respects the flow of language rather than submitting to the law of the box. Despite its advantages, however, the flush left format is frought with danger. Above all, the designer must work hard to control the appearance of the *rag* along the left edge. A good rag looks pleasantly uneven, with no lines that are excessively long or short, and with hyphenation kept to an absolute minimum. A rag is considered "bad" when it looks too even (or too uneven), or when it begins to form regular shapes, like wedges, moons, or diving boards.

JUSTIFIED
The left and right edges are both even.

When it is good: Justified text makes a clean, figural shape on the page. Its efficient use of space makes it the norm for newspapers and books of continuous text.

When it is evil: Ugly gaps can occur as text is forced into lines of even measure. Avoid this by making sure the line length is long enough in relation to the size of type. As the font gets smaller, more words will fit on each line.

FLUSH LEFT/RAGGED RIGHT
The left edge is hard, and the right edge is soft.

When it is good: Designers choose to set text flush left when they want to respect the organic flow of language and avoid the uneven spacing that plagues narrow columns of justified type.

When it is evil: The flush left column loses its organic appearance when disgraced with a "bad rag." Strive vigilantly to create the illusion of a random, natural edge without yielding to the sin of hyphenation.

Ugly gaps appear when the designer has made the line length too short, or the author has selected words that are too
l   o   n   g   .

TYPE CRIME:
FULL OF HOLES
A column that is too narrow is full of gaps.

A bad rag will fall into weird shapes along the right edge, instead of looking random.

TYPE CRIME:
BAD RAG
An ugly wedge-shape spoils the ragged edge.

Flush right/ragged left is a variant of the more familiar flush left setting. It is common wisdom among typographers that flush right text is hard to read, because it forces the reader's eye to find a new position at the start of each line. This could be true, or it could be an urban legend. At any rate, the flush right setting is rarely employed for long bodies of text. Used in smaller blocks, however, flush right text forms effective marginal notes, sidebars, pull quotes, or other passages that comment on a main body or image. A flush or ragged edge can suggest attraction (or repulsion) between chunks of information.

Centered text is symmetrical,
like the facade of a classical building.
Centered type is often employed on
invitations, title pages, certificates, and tomb stones.
The edges of a centered column
are allowed to be dramatically uneven.
Centered lines are often broken to emphasize a key phrase
(such as the name of the bride
or the date of her wedding)
or to allow a new thought to begin on its own line.
Breaking lines in this manner is called
breaking for sense.

FLUSH RIGHT/RAGGED LEFT
*The right edge is hard, and
the left edge is soft.*

When it is good: Flush right text can be a welcome departure from the familiar. It makes effective captions, sidebars, and marginal notes, suggesting affinities among elements on the page.

When it is evil: Flush right text can be an unwelcome departure from the familiar, annoying cautious readers. Bad rags can threaten flush right text just as they afflict flush left, with the added difficulty that punctuation at the ends of lines can weaken the hard right edge.

CENTERED
*Uneven lines are centered between
the left and right edges.*

When it is good: Centered text is formal and classical, bearing rich associations with history and tradition. It invites the designer to break a text for sense and create an organic shape in response to the flow of content.

When it is evil: Centered text is static and conventional. Used without care, it looks stodgy, static, and mournful, like a tombstone.

Lots of punctuation (at the ends of lines) will attack, threaten, and generally weaken the flush right edge. Watch out for this.

TYPE CRIME:
PUNCTUATION EATS
THE EDGE
*This is not a true crime
so much as a situation
of compromise.*

REST
IN
PEACE

*Death is not a crime,
and neither is centered
type. Embrace the
staid formality of this
setting with caution,
however.*

Louise But designers do the same thing,
don't they? They often sell themselves
with impressive statements that don't really
fit the facts of what they make.

BEYOND NOSTALGIA

Embroidery, woodcarving, and minutely detailed ceramic glazes are not techniques we usually associate with contemporary art and design. These age-old methods nonetheless play a prominent part in the work of several current artists and designers, including Berend Strik, Wim Delvoye, and Hella Jongerius.

Berend Strik's work resembles an amalgam of modern vulgar culture, old crafts, and new subject matter. For one of his best-known pieces (*Untitled*, 1993), Strik pasted gaping female mouths in a row, cut away a similar number of phalluses, and accentuated the lip outlines with elegant lines of cross stitching and other ornamental embroidery. The modification tempts the spectator away from the obvious pornographic interpretation so that, suddenly, the strains of a heavenly choir seem to emerge from those unmistakably lubricious lips. The publication of French philosopher Georges Bataille's book *Les larmes d'Eros* (1986) has made us aware of just how far religious ecstasy is intertwined with sexuality, death, and violence. Strik's subject is the same. His quaint embroidery technique challenges the hypocrisy with which past

HELLA JONGERIUS
Book, 2003
Designers: COMA, Amsterdam/New York
Author: Louise Schouwenberg
Publisher: Phaidon
Photograph: Dan Meyers

I looked into the form without really knowing it at first; I saw walls flying across space. The tilting planes climbed and cut into each other, violent, shattering any notion of building in the conventional sense.

And the dialogue began between Daniel Libeskind and myself, how could such a form be built?

Libeskind took me back to ancient times, to the Pyramids. We talked of stone and how to build a form like this from masonry – but the oblique planes and large spans would have needed huge 'strapping' with prestress or numerous tie devices. Attractive as the idea was in its primitive urges, I advocated concrete or steel to maintain the daring alignments.

There were two ways to consider the question:

implant a certain massiveness and celebrate a high redundancy in the configuration;

or trap the tilting planes in a modern rationale of discrete 'framing'.

The former would give concrete as a material of tradition, used in an extreme definition; the latter would reduce the great planes to a framing buttressed by internal stiffeners and cross bracing. One method provides density, opacity, and three-dimensional surface as structure, the other lightness and openness that is then clad and windowed. The first answer leads to a labyrinth, the second to transparency.

We exchanged metaphors.

If the form were closed, it could be a mineral deposit, or if an open transparent steel framed building, it could be a lantern or a beacon. If it were heavy, could it be hacked out of granite, or was it buildable out of special masonry? The images helped loosen the thinking and inspired us to look for the radical.

193

INFORMAL
Book, 2002
Designer: Januzzi Smith
Author: Cecil Balmond
Publisher: Prestel
Photograph: Dan Meyers
This book is a manifesto for an "informal" approach to structural engineering and architecture. Throughout the book, the typography combines flush left and flush right alignments, creating a tiny but insistent seam or fissure inside the text column, and irregular rags on the outer edges. This construction beautifully expresses the principle of informality, underscored by the integration of sketches with the typography of the book.

 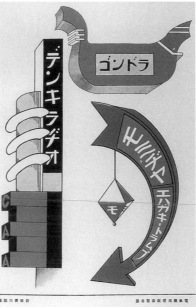

LU FRAN MOTEL
(FAR LEFT)
Wildwood, New Jersey
Photographer:
Dorothy Kresz

ILLUMINATED SIGNS
(LEFT)
Japan, 1924

*Commercial signs
often employ stacks
of characters.*

SHELF OF SPINES
*Stacked letters sometimes
appear on the spines of books,
but vertical baselines are more
common. Starting from the
top and reading down is the
predominant direction,
especially in the U.S.*

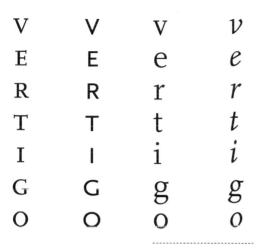

SMALL CAPS, STACKED

TYPE CRIME:
STACKED LOWERCASE

SCALA LOWERCASE, VERTICAL BASELINES
top to bottom   bottom to top   both directions

STACKED CAPITALS
Roman letters are designed to sit side by side, not on top of one another. Uppercase letters form more stable stacks than lowercase letters. Centering the column helps to even out the differences in width. (The letter *I* is a perennial problem.)

STACKED LOWERCASE
Stacks of lowercase letters are especially awkward because the ascenders and descenders make the vertical spacing appear uneven, and the varied width of the characters makes the stacks look precarious.

VERTICAL BASELINES
The simplest way to make a line of text form a vertical line is to change the orientation of the baseline from horizontal to vertical. This preserves the natural affinity among letters sitting on a line.

There is no fixed rule determining whether type should run from top to bottom or from bottom to top. It is more common, however, especially in the U.S., to run text on the spines of books from top to bottom. (You can also run text up and down simultaneously.)

English is not Chinese. John Kane, 2002

Aspekte zeitgenössischer
Kunst aus dem Elsaß
Teil 1: 17.05. bis 06.07.97

Parallelen im Schnittpunkt

Carrefour de Parallèles

Aspects de l'art
contemporain d'Alsace
Section 1: 17.05. bis 06.07.97

Badischer
Kunstverein

PARALLELEN IM
SCHNITTPUNKT
(CROSSING PARALLELS)
Posters, 1997
Designer: Gerwin Schmidt
Publisher: Art-Club Karlsruhe
The axes of type and landscape
intersect to create these posters
that are simple, powerful, and
direct. The type is mirrored in
German and French.

HIERARCHY	Hierarchy	HIERARCHY		HIERARCHY
I Division of angels	Division of angels	DIVISION OF ANGELS		*angel*
A. Angel	Angel	*Angel*		*archangel*
B. Archangel	Archangel	*Archangel*	DIVISION	*cherubim*
C. Cherubim	Cherubim	*Cherubim*	OF ANGELS	*seraphim*
D. Seraphim	Seraphim	*Seraphim*		
II Ruling body of clergy	Ruling body of clergy	RULING BODY OF CLERGY		*pope*
A. Pope	Pope	*Pope*		*cardinal*
B. Cardinal	Cardinal	*Cardinal*	RULING BODY	*archbishop*
C. Archbishop	Archbishop	*Archbishop*	OF CLERGY	*bishop*
D. Bishop	Bishop	*Bishop*		
III Parts of a text	Parts of a text	PARTS OF A TEXT		*work*
A. Work	Work	*Work*		*chapter*
B. Chapter	Chapter	*Chapter*	PARTS OF	*section*
C. Section	Section	*Section*	A TEXT	*subsection*
D. Subsection	Subsection	*Subsection*		

SYMBOLS, INDENTS, AND LINE BREAKS	INDENTS AND LINE BREAKS ONLY	FONT CHANGE, INDENTS, AND LINE BREAKS	ALIGNMENT, FONT CHANGE, AND LINE BREAKS

HIERARCHY A typographic *hierarchy* expresses an organizational system for content, emphasizing some data and diminishing others. A hierarchy helps readers scan a text, knowing where to enter and exit and how to pick and choose among its offerings. Each level of the hierarchy should be signaled by one or more cues, applied consistently across a body of text. A cue can be spatial (indent, line spacing, placement on page) or graphic (size, style, color of typeface). Infinite variations are possible.

REDUNDANCY Writers are generally trained to avoid redundancy, as in the expressions "future plans" or "past history." In typography, some redundancy is acceptable, even recommended. For example, paragraphs are traditionally marked with a line break *and* an indent, a redundancy that has proven quite practical, as each signal provides backup for the other. To create an elegant economy of signals, try using no more than three cues for each level or break in a document.

BOLD, ITALIC, UNDERLINED CAPS!

CREATING EMPHASIS WITHIN RUNNING TEXT Emphasizing a word or phrase within a body of text usually requires only one signal. *Italic* is the standard form of emphasis. There are many alternatives, however, including **boldface**, SMALL CAPS, or a change in color. You can also create emphasis with a **different font**; a full-range type family such as Scala has many font variations designed to work together. If you want to mix font families, such as Scala and **Futura**, adjust the sizes so that the x-heights align.

MAIN HEAD ——————— COMMON TYPOGRAPHIC DISEASES

MAIN TEXT ——————— Various forms of dysfunction appear among populations exposed to typography for long periods of time. Listed here are a number of frequently observed afflictions.

TYPOPHILIA An excessive attachment to and fascination with the shape of letters, often to the exclusion of other interests and object choices. Typophiliacs usually die penniless and alone.

TYPOPHOBIA The irrational dislike of letterforms, often marked by a preference for icons, dingbats, and—in fatal cases—bullets and daggers. The fears of the typophobe can often be quieted (but not cured) by steady doses of Helvetica and Times Roman.

SUBSECTIONS ——————— TYPOCHONDRIA A persistent anxiety that one has selected the wrong typeface. This condition is often paired with OKD (optical kerning disorder), the need to constantly adjust and readjust the spaces between letters.

TYPOTHERMIA The promiscuous refusal to make a lifelong commitment to a single typeface—or even to five or six, as some doctors recommend. The *typothermiac* is constantly tempted to test drive "hot" new fonts, often without a proper license.

COMMON TYPOGRAPHIC DISEASES

There are endless ways to express the hierarchy of a document.

Various forms of dysfunction appear among populations exposed to typography for long periods of time. Listed here are a number of frequently observed afflictions.

Typophilia An excessive attachment to and fascination with the shape of letters, often to the exclusion of other interests and object choices. Typophiliacs usually die penniless and alone.

Typophobia The irrational dislike of letterforms, often marked by a preference for icons, dingbats, and—in fatal cases—bullets and daggers. The fears of the typophobe can often be quieted (but not cured) by steady doses of Helvetica and Times Roman.

Typochondria A persistent anxiety that one has selected the wrong typeface. This condition is often paired with OKD (optical kerning disorder), the need to constantly adjust and readjust the spaces between letters.

Typothermia The promiscuous refusal to make a lifelong commitment to a single typeface—or even to five or six, as some doctors recommend. The *typothermiac* is constantly tempted to test drive "hot" new fonts, often without a proper license.

zur Huldigung des Kaisers abgebildet:

„Ich habe es nicht gewollt."

Bei Soissons wurden die feindlichen Reih'n
Von den tapfern Deutschen geschlagen,
Da stellt nach der Schlacht Kaiser Wilhelm sich ein,
Um den Helden ein Dankwort zu sagen.

Und wo der geliebte Herrscher erscheint,
Erheben sich grüßend die Hände.
Aus tausend kräftigen Stimmen vereint
Gab's ein Jubelgeschrei ohne Ende.

Nachdem schritt der Kaiser, der sichtlich bewegt,
Auf das Feld, wo vor wenigen Stunden
Die Helden zur ewigen Ruh' man gelegt,
Die den Tod auf dem Schlachtfeld gefunden.

Am Grab eines Jünglings stand der Kaiser gebannt—
Kaum „Siebzehn" — im Grab bei den Alten. —
Der Herrscher von Wehmut jetzt übermannt
Konnt' der Tränen sich nicht mehr enthalten.

Er betete Worte kerndeutsch — treu wie Gold,
Vor denen ein Weltall sich beuge:
„Gott Vater im Himmel — ich hab's nicht gewollt.
Du weißt es — Du bist mein Zeuge."

Paul Hambrock
Oberleutnant a. D.

Mit Genehmigung des Generalkommandos.

Karl Kraus zählt Wilhelm II. zu „den Schwerverbrechern auf dem Thron" mit der „Beteuerung, daß sie es nicht gewollt haben, woran sie, da sie es taten, doch schuldig sind" [F 595,2].

1920; F 531,52f.

→ gemeinsames **Vorgehen**
→ etwas zum **Vortrag** bringen
→ in die **Falle** gehen
→ ich habe alles reiflich **erwogen**
→ im **Lauf** des Abends
→ ein **Laut** auf den Lippen
→ zum **Schluß**
→ zu **Mantua** in Banden Der treue Hofer war
→ **Gesellschaft** mit beschränkter Haftung / G. m. b. H.
→ **vorlieb** nehmen

— — (Momentan sind wir z. B. bei der seit der Thronbesteigung!) — —

— — So erlebte ich, daß er einen doch i[...] Major, den Adjutanten des Kronprinzen, ga[...] Ohr zog, ihm einen tüchtigen Schlag[...] gab und sagte: — —

— — empfing er in Tempelhof im Sal[...] minister und den Chef des Militärkabinettes mi[...] alten Esel glaubt, daß ihr alles besser wiß[...]

*) Deutsche Verlagsanstalt, Stuttgart, 192[...]

Und daß das »gemeinsame Vorgehen« für den[...] war, »sobald Kraus die Satire auf Kaiser Wilhelm[...] werde«, beweist eine Vertrautheit der Innsb[...] Programm, die ich selbst am Nachmittag noch n[...] ihnen in die Falle gegangen! Aber wenn einer[...] Innsbruck auf Demonstrationen ausgehen, bis[...] Abends eine Ahnung von dem Vorhandensein[...] will ich dem Wilhelm glauben, daß er es nicht ge[...] Josef, daß er alles reiflich erwogen hat. Die Wa[...] einer vagen Kenntnis meiner Gesinnung, aber v[...] die ihre auszuleben, in den Saal geführten Ind[...] Abends ein Dutzend weit besserer Anlässe — e[...] zwei Diebsgenerale — hatten vorübergehen lass[...] der Laut auf den Lippen erstarb, und erst zum[...] über die eigene Unregsamkeit ihnen Bewußts[...] ihre Anwesenheit legitimierten, indem sie[...]

WÖRTERBUCH DER REDENSARTEN/
KARL KRAUS, DIE FACKEL
Book, 1999
Designer: Anne Burdick
Publisher: Österreichischen Akademie der Wissenschaften
*This book presents essays from the journal Die Fackel,
published by the Viennese writer Karl Kraus from 1899 to 1936.
The journal's text appears in the center of each page. This text is
sometimes represented with an image of the original publication
and sometimes filtered through the modern typography of the new
edition. In the beige-colored margins, different styles and sizes of
type indicate different modes of editorial commentary.*

Speak Up

UPDATES, NEWS & ANNOUNCEMENTS

New Business Article: Pro-Bono or No-Bono | **Three new** Word Its

A DIVISION OF UNDER CONSIDERATION   AUTHORS   ABOUT   CONTACT

Interviews   ⟡ SEE ALL

Most Recent
> **NEW** Andrew Blauvelt
> Claude Garamond
> David Carson

Book Reviews   ⟡ SEE ALL

Most Recent
> Kyle Cooper
> Project M – Vol. 1
> I am Almost Always Hungry

News and Events   ⟡ SEE ALL

Most Recent
> Mister Retro Launches
> The Brand Gap: A One-Day Workshop
> Keywording with FontShop

Essays   ⟡ SEE ALL

Interested in writing an essay for Speak Up? Inquire within

Business Resources   ⟡ SEE ALL

Most Recent
> Pro-Bono or No-Bono
> Spec Work Arithmetic
> A Dozen Common Mistakes

Open Space   ⟡ SEE ALL

Most Recent
> Brook Lorntson
> Paul Kimball
> Arturo Elenes

Join our Mailing List

E-mail (Required)

[   ]

Your Name (Required)

[   ]

⟨sign me up⟩

¿Es el Diseño Gráfico Universal?

Discussion

Is graphic design a universal language? As the face of the United States changes, how do designers fit into the growing language challenges? For instance, the new light rail system in Minneapolis has ticket machines that have instructions in four languages: English, Spanish, Somali and Hmong.

Continue reading this entry

By brook on Feb.20.2004 › Link › Comments [12]

Andrew Blauvelt Speaks Up

Interview

Can graphic design save itself? What exactly do we need to save ourselves from? Questions like these plagued me after reading Andrew Blauvelt's essay in Emigre #64 *Towards Critical Autonomy or Can Graphic Design Save Itself?* This wasn't the first time Blauvelt's writing had incited me. *Building Bridges: A Research Agenda for Education and Practice* called for a refinement of graduate study and practice in graphic design. We should push beyond the limits already experienced. And that's where his Emigre article put a bigger fire under me. Change what we do, not how we do it. It's more about point of view than visualizing your point, with a great opportunity for revolutionary work. Obvious? For me it wasn't.

> Read the interview.

By Jason on Feb.19.2004 › Link › Comments [3]

Are There Too Many Of Us?

Discussion

Going to a bar or a coffee shop these days, it seems like the city is overrun by art directors, designers and other creative professionals. It used to be that when you stated to be a graphic designer, it was perceived as exotic and even special and people looked at you with the "ah, that explains it" type of look. Now everyone seems to be in the creative field. And I don't think I frequent spots that are considered designer-hang-outs. However, I live and work in Los Angeles and what happens here might not be the norm for the rest of the country, but I noticed the same in Switzerland, where I grew up and went through art school. Maybe not to the extent as here in southern California, but still, the shift is significant.

Continue reading this entry

By Peter Scherrer on Feb.18.2004 › Link › Comments [112]

Recent Comments

> ¿Es el Diseño Gráfico Universal? [12]
> Are There Too Many Of Us? [112]
> A Rewarding Experience [9]
> Andrew Blauvelt Speaks Up [3]
> The Icky Mouse Club [35]
> My Name is Font. *Ultra* Pixel Font. [36]
> Design: Alive and Well, and Living in the Midwest [27]
> A Branded Education [28]

Search

Enter Keywords

[   ]

⟨go find it!⟩

Word It › Tease   ⟡ SEE ALL

by: Kiran Max Weber

Most Recent
> Tease
> Empty
> Virtue

Archives

[By Category   ▼]

[By Month   ▼]

Submit an Idea for Discussion

E-mail (Required)

[   ]

SPEAK UP (LEFT)
Web site, 2004
Designer: Armin Vit; logo by Michael Clark
This on-line design forum presents readers with a dense menu of content articulated into a clear hierarchy. Each type of content is labeled (interview, discussion, essay). Featured threads are presented at the center of the screen, where a substantial passage of text allows readers to decide whether to proceed further. Titles are given drama and importance through placement, color, and font choice. Site branding is kept to a minimum, allowing the content to dominate.

Most Web sites are controlled by hierarchies in an even more systematic way than print documents. A site's file structure proceeds from a root down to directories holding various levels of content. An HTML page contains a hierarchy of elements that can be nested one inside the other. The site's organization is reflected in its interface—from navigation to the formatting of content. Typography helps elucidate the hierarchies governing all these features.

Dynamic Web sites use databases to build pages on the fly as users search for specific content. Databases cut across the planned hierarchy of a site, bringing up links from different levels and content areas—or from other Web sites. Typographic style sheets are used to weight the information gathered, helping users find what they need.

βeta A9   Search: | Ellen Lupton | GO |

Home   Sign In

Hello, sign in to enable site features.

Web Results [close]   Showing 1 - 10 of about 7,270

Ellen Lupton: New Home Page
Think more, design less. Announcements. Archive, This site is an informal archive and design resource drawn from the work of **Ellen Lupton** and Abbott Miller. ...
http://www.designwritingresearch.org/ - 4k Cached
(Site Info)

Design Writing Research: Ellen Lupton
About us, **Ellen Lupton** is a writer, curator, and graphic designer. She is director of the MFA program in graphic design at Maryland ...
http://www.designwritingresearch.org/lupton_page.html - 5k Cached (Site Info)

: : Speak Up > Ellen Lupton › "Thinking With Design" : :
... **Ellen Lupton** › "Thinking With Design". **Ellen Lupton** To Present "Thinking With Design". **Ellen Lupton**, curator, graphic designer ...
http://www.underconsideration.com/speakup/archives/

Book Results [close]   Showing 1 - 10 of about 470

Design Writing Research
by Ellen Lupton (10 June, 1999)

Skin: Surface, Substance, and Design
by Ellen Lupton, Jennifer Tobias, Alicia Imperiale, Grace Jeffers, and Randi Mates (March, 2002)

Design Culture Now: The National Design Triennial
by Donald Albrecht, Ellen Lupton, Steven Holt, and Steven Skov Holt (15 March, 2000)

Mixing Messages: Graphic Design In Contemporary Culture
by Ellen Lupton (September, 1996)

Letters from the Avant-Garde: Modern Graphic Design
by Ellen Lupton and Elaine Lustig Cohen (March, 1996)

Open Search History

WWW.A9.COM, Search engine, 2004
A search engines applies a typographic hierarchy to the results it calls up, using color, size, weight, and underlining to differentiate its parts.

Many designers are passionately committed to building accessible sites for the Web. This medium was invented in order to provide universal access to information, a goal it may some day achieve, regardless of a user's physical abilities or access to specialized software.

Cascading Style Sheets (CSS) allow designers to plan alternate layouts depending on the user's software and hardware. For example, cell phones and personal digital assistants display Web sites in a text-only format, while some users have outdated browsers or lack the software "plug-ins" required for displaying certain kinds of files. Style sheets can also be used to design print-friendly versions of interactive documents.

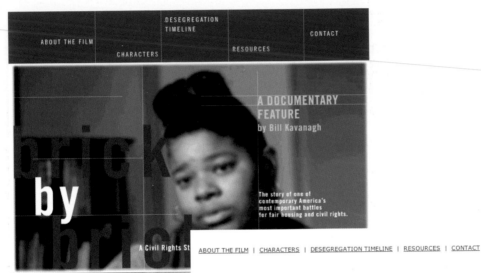

BRICK-BY-BRICK.ORG
Web site, 2001
Designers: Red Canoe
Publisher: Kavanagh Productions
This Flash-enabled site was created for a documentary film about desegregation. It includes a text-based, HTML version, designed for users without access to Flash. The HTML version is also easy to print and is useful to journalists or researchers desiring direct access to the text.

Brick by Brick: a civil rights story is a documentary by Bill Kavanagh. It tells the story of one of contemporary America's most important battles for fair housing and civil rights.

[This Web site is the text-only version of Brick-by-Brick.com. Use this page for easy reading and printing. Please visit the graphics-rich site if your browser supports graphics and the Macromedia Flash 5 player. We recommend that you upgrade your browser to view the graphics-rich site and most other modern Web content. You can upgrade your browsers at either Microsoft (Internet Explorer) or Netscape.]

ABOUT THE FILM

Synopsis
Bill Kavanagh's *Brick by Brick: A Civil Rights Story* is a feature-length documentary that follows three families in Yonkers, NY through a winding path as they confront city politics of racial division and work to change their hometown. The film follows a decade-long struggle over desegregation in a contemporary northern locale.

The film deals with the isolation of people of color in an institutionally created public housing ghetto, and the segregated schools in this community. *Brick by Brick: A Civil Rights Story* goes on to document the progress of community action to improve schools and finally a federal suit filed to force the city to act.

Visually impaired users employ automated screen readers that "linearize" Web pages into a continuous text that can be read aloud by a machine. Techniques for achieving accessibility include the captioning of all layout tables (or, better yet, the avoidance of tables altogether), the consistent use of "alt tags" (which identify image files), and the placement of page anchors in front of repeated navigation elements that enable users to go directly to the main content. Various software programs allow designers to test the linearization of their pages.

CLAPHAMINSTITUTE.ORG
Web site, 2003
Designer: Colin Day, Exclamation Communications
Publisher: The Clapham Institute
This site was designed to be accessible to sighted and non-sighted users. At right is a linearized version of the page above.

One of the defining principles of the Web is that it should provide all people, regardless of physical or technological readiness, with access to information. Patrick Lynch and Sarah Horton, 2001

PARAGRAPHS do not occur in nature. Whereas sentences are grammatical elements intrinsic to the spoken language, paragraphs are a wholly literary convention designed to divide content into portions that are more appetizing to readers (and writers) than an endless stream of discourse. In the seventeenth century, it became standard to mark the beginning of a new paragraph with an indent, and to mark its close with a line break. Before then, typographers sometimes left extra space between paragraphs or sentences (without a line break), preserving the clean edges of the text block. Despite the ubiquity of the indent/line break convention today, numerous alternatives can be used in its place. Inventing new ones is an intriguing typographic exercise.

This exercise indebted to George Sadek and William Bevington at the Cooper Union

For the glorye of the sayntes whiche shal be yeuen at the last comyng shal neuer ende ne fynysshe. And to this signyfy- aunce the first responce of the first weke of aduent hath iiii verse to rekene ☾ Gloria patri & filio for one to the reporte of the iiii wekis, and how be it that there be iiii comynges of our lord, yet the chirche maketh mencion in especial but of tweyne, that is to wete, of that he came in humayne nature to the world, and of that he cometh to the Jugement & dome, as it apperith in thoffyce of the chirche of this tyme. And therfor the fas- tynges that ben in this tyme, ben of gladnes and of joye in one partie, & that other partie is in bitternesse of herte. By cause of the comynge of our lorde in our nature humayne, they ben of joye and gladnes. And by cause of the comyng at the day of Jugement they be of bitternes and heuynes.

BIBLIA INNOCENTIUM
Page detail, 1892
Designer: William Morris
Publisher: Kelmscott Press
William Morris admired the dense pages of the early Renaissance. Here, he has used a paragraph symbol in place of line breaks and indents.

The table is covered with a table cloth which itself is protected by a plastic table cloth. Drapes and double drapes are at the windows. We have carpets, slipcovers, coasters, wainscoting, lampshades. Each trinket sits on a doily, each flower in its pot, and each pot in its saucer.

Everything is protected and surrounded. Even in the garden, each cluster is encircled with wire netting, each path is outlined by bricks, mosaics, or flagstones.

This could be analyzed as an anxious sequestration, as an obsessional symbolism: the obsession of the cottage owner and small capitalist not only to possess, but to underline what he possesses two or three times. There, as other places, the unconscious speaks in the redundancy of signs, in their con- notations and overworking.

— *Jean Baudrillard, 1969*

INDENT AND LINE BREAK

The table is covered with a table cloth which itself is protected by a plastic table cloth. Drapes and double drapes are at the windows. We have carpets, slipcovers, coasters, wainscoting, lampshades. Each trinket sits on a doily, each flower in its pot, and each pot in its saucer.

Everything is protected and surrounded. Even in the garden, each cluster is encircled with wire netting, each path is out- lined by bricks, mosaics, or flagstones.

This could be analyzed as an anxious sequestration, as an obsessional symbolism: the obsession of the cottage owner and small capitalist not only to possess, but to underline what he possesses two or three times. There, as other places, the unconscious speaks in the redundancy of signs, in their connotations and overworking.

— *Jean Baudrillard, 1969*

OUTDENT, OR HANGING INDENTATION

The table is covered with a table cloth which itself is protected by a plastic table cloth. Drapes and double drapes are at the windows. We have carpets, slipcovers, coasters, wainscoting, lampshades. Each trinket sits on a doily, each flower in its pot, and each pot in its saucer.
Everything is protected and surrounded. Even in the garden, each cluster is encircled with wire netting, each path is outlined by bricks, mosaics, or flagstones.
This could be analyzed as an anxious sequestration, as an obsessional symbolism: the obsession of the cottage owner and small capitalist not only to possess, but to underline what he possesses two or three times. There, as other places, the unconscious speaks in the redundancy of signs, in their connotations and overworking.

— *Jean Baudrillard, 1969*

LINE BREAK ONLY, WITHOUT INDENT

The table is covered with a table cloth which itself is protected by a plastic table cloth. Drapes and double drapes are at the windows. We have carpets, slipcovers, coasters, wainscoting, lampshades. Each trinket sits on a doily, each flower in its pot, and each pot in its saucer.   Everything is protected and surrounded. Even in the garden, each cluster is encircled with wire netting, each path is outlined by bricks, mosaics, or flagstones.   This could be analyzed as an anxious sequestration, as an obsessional symbolism: the obsession of the cottage owner and small capitalist not only to possess, but to underline what he possesses two or three times. There, as other places, the unconscious speaks in the redundancy of signs, in their connotations and overworking.

— *Jean Baudrillard, 1969*

EXTRA SPACE INSIDE LINE, WITHOUT LINE BREAK

The table is covered with a table cloth which itself is protected by a plastic table cloth. Drapes and double drapes are at the windows. We have carpets, slipcovers, coasters, wainscoting, lampshades. Each trinket sits on a doily, each flower in its pot, and each pot in its saucer.

Everything is protected and surrounded. Even in the garden, each cluster is encircled with wire netting, each path is outlined by bricks, mosaics, or flagstones.

This could be analyzed as an anxious sequestration, as an obsessional symbolism: the obsession of the cottage owner and small capitalist not only to possess, but to underline what he possesses two or three times. There, as other places, the unconscious speaks in the redundancy of signs, in their connotations and overworking.

— *Jean Baudrillard, 1969*

LINE BREAK AND 1/2 LINE SPACE

The table is covered with a table cloth which itself is protected by a plastic table cloth. Drapes and double drapes are at the windows. We have carpets, slipcovers, coasters, wainscoting, lampshades. Each trinket sits on a doily, each flower in its pot, and each pot in its saucer. ■ Everything is protected and surrounded. Even in the garden, each cluster is encircled with wire netting, each path is outlined by bricks, mosaics, or flagstones. ■ This could be analyzed as an anxious sequestration, as an obsessional symbolism: the obsession of the cottage owner and small capitalist not only to possess, but to underline what he possesses two or three times. There, as other places, the unconscious speaks in the redundancy of signs, in their connotations and overworking.

— *Jean Baudrillard, 1969*

SYMBOL; NO INDENT OR LINE BREAK

The first word of the first line is *the* critical word of that particular body of text. Let it start flush, at least. W. A. Dwiggins

You can express the meaning of a word or an idea through the spacing, sizing, and placement of letters on the page. Designers often think this way when creating logotypes, posters, or editorial headlines. In this project, physical processes such as disruption, expansion, and migration are expressed through the spacing and arrangement of letters. The round *Os* in Futura make it a fun typeface to use for this project.

Examples of student work from
Maryland Institute College of Art

sition   transiti

JOHNSCHEN KUDOS

disruption   c o m pression

JOHNSCHEN KUDOS   JOHNSCHEN KUDOS

ion

t

a

e e x p p**expansion** i o o n n

iǵ

migra**tion**

MARCOS KOLTHAR   JASON HOGG

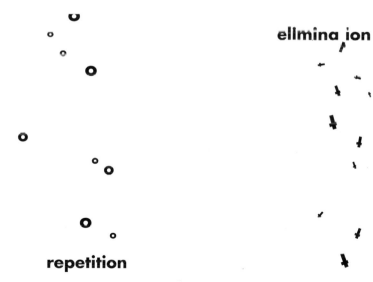

e**llmina ion**

repetition

HEATHER WILLIAMS   HEATHER WILLIAMS

Use modes of alignment (flush left, flush right, justified, and centered) to actively interpret a passage of text. The passage here, from Walter Ong's book *Orality and Literacy: The Technologizing of the Word*, explains how the invention of printing with movable type imposed a new spatial order on the written word, in contrast with the more organic pages of the manuscript era. Each project comments on the conflicts between hard and soft, industrial and natural, planning and randomness, that underlie all typographic composition.

Examples of student work from Maryland Institute College of Art

PRINT SITUATES WORDS IN SPACE MORE RELENTLESSLY THAN WRITING EVER DID. writing moves words the sound world from BUT PRINT LOCKS WORDS INTO to a world of visual space, POSITION IN THIS SPACE. CONTROL OF POSITION IS EVERYTHING IN PRINT. PRINTED TEXTS LOOK MACHINE-MADE, AS THEY ARE. in handwriting, control of space tends to be ornamental, TYPOGRAPHIC CONTROL TYPICALLY IMPRESSES MOST BY ITS TIDINESS ornate, as in calligraphy. AND INVISIBILITY: THE LINES PERFECTLY REGULAR, ALL JUSTIFIED ON THE RIGHT SIDE, EVERYTHING COMING OUT EVEN VISUALLY, AND WITHOUT THE AID OF GUIDELINES OR RULED BORDERS THAT OFTEN OCCUR IN MANUSCRIPTS. THIS IS AN INSISTENT WORLD OF COLD, NON-HUMAN, FACTS.

Randomly spaced words break free from a rigidly justified column.
LU ZHANG

PRINT

situates words in space more relentlessly

than writing ever did. Control of position

is everything in print. Printed texts look

machine-made, as they are. Typographic

control typically impresses most by its

WRITING　　　tidiness and invisibility: the lines perfectly

moves words from the sound world　regular, all justified on the right side,

to a world of visual space,　everything coming out even visually, and

but print locks words　without the aid of guidelines or ruled

into position in this space.　borders that often occur in manuscripts.

In handwriting, control of space　This is an insistent world of cold,

tends to be ornamental, ornate,　non-human, facts.

as in calligraphy.

Passages of flush left and flush right text hinge from a central axis.
JOHNSCHEN KUDOS

Print situates words
in space more
relentlessly than
writing ever did.
Writing moves words from the sound world to a world of visual space,
but print locks
words into position
in this space.
Control of position
is everything in
print. Printed texts
look machine-
made, as they are.
In handwriting, control of space tends to be ornamental, ornate.
Typographic control
typically impresses
most by its tidiness
and invisibility: the
lines perfectly regular,
all justified on the
right side, everything　This is an insistent
coming out even　world of cold,
visually, and without　non-human, facts.
the aid of guidelines
or ruled borders that
often occur in
manuscripts.

Long, centered lines are bridges between narrow, ragged columns.
BENJAMIN LUTZ

relentlessly than writing ever did. Writing moves words from the sound world to a world of visual space, but print locks words into position in this space. Control of position is everything in print. Printed texts look machine-made, as they are. In handwriting, control of space tends to be ornamental, ornate, as in calligraphy. Typographic control typically impresses most by its tidiness and invisibility; the lines perfectly regular, all justified on the right side, everything coming out even visually, and without the aid of guidelines or ruled borders that often occur in manuscripts. This is an insistent world of cold, non-human, facts.

Print situates words in space more

Print situates words in space more relentlessly than writing ever did. Writing moves words from the sound world to a world of visual space, but print locks words into position in this space.

Control of position is everything in print. Printed texts look machine-made, as they are. In handwriting, control of space tends to be ornamental, ornate, as in calligraphy. Typographic control typically impresses most by its tidiness and invisibility; the lines perfectly regular, all justified on the right side, everything coming out even visually, and without the aid of guidelines or ruled borders that often occur in manuscripts, THIS IS AN INSISTENT WORLD OF COLD, NON-HUMAN, FACTS.

The beginning of the paragraph is moved to the end.
DANIEL ARBELLO

A single line slides out of a justified block.
KAPILA CHASE

Print situates words in space more relentlessly than writing ever did.

Writing moves words from the sound world to a world of

V I S U A L   S P A C E

but print locks words into position in this space. Control of position is everything in print. Printed texts look machine-made, as they are.

In handwriting, control of space tends to be ornamental, ornate, as in calligraphy.

Typographic control typically impresses most by its tidiness and invisibility; the lines perfectly regular, all justified on the right side, everything coming out even visually, and without the aid of guidelines or ruled borders that often occur in manuscripts.

This is an insistent world of cold, non-human, facts.

Print situates words in space more relentlessly than writing ever did. Writing moves words from the

sound world to a world of visual space, but print locks words into position in this space.

Control of position is everything in print. Printed texts look

machine-made, as they are. In handwriting, control of space tends to be

ornamental, ornate, as in calligraphy. Typographic control typically impresses most

by its tidiness and invisibility: the lines perfectly regular, all justified on the right side,

everything coming out even visually, and without the aid of guidelines or ruled borders

that often occur in manuscripts. This is an insistent world of cold, non-human, facts.

Elements break away from a justified column.
EFRAT LEVUSH

Text is forced into a grid of ragged squares.
KIM BENDER

SPRING 1995. HALTER DRESS

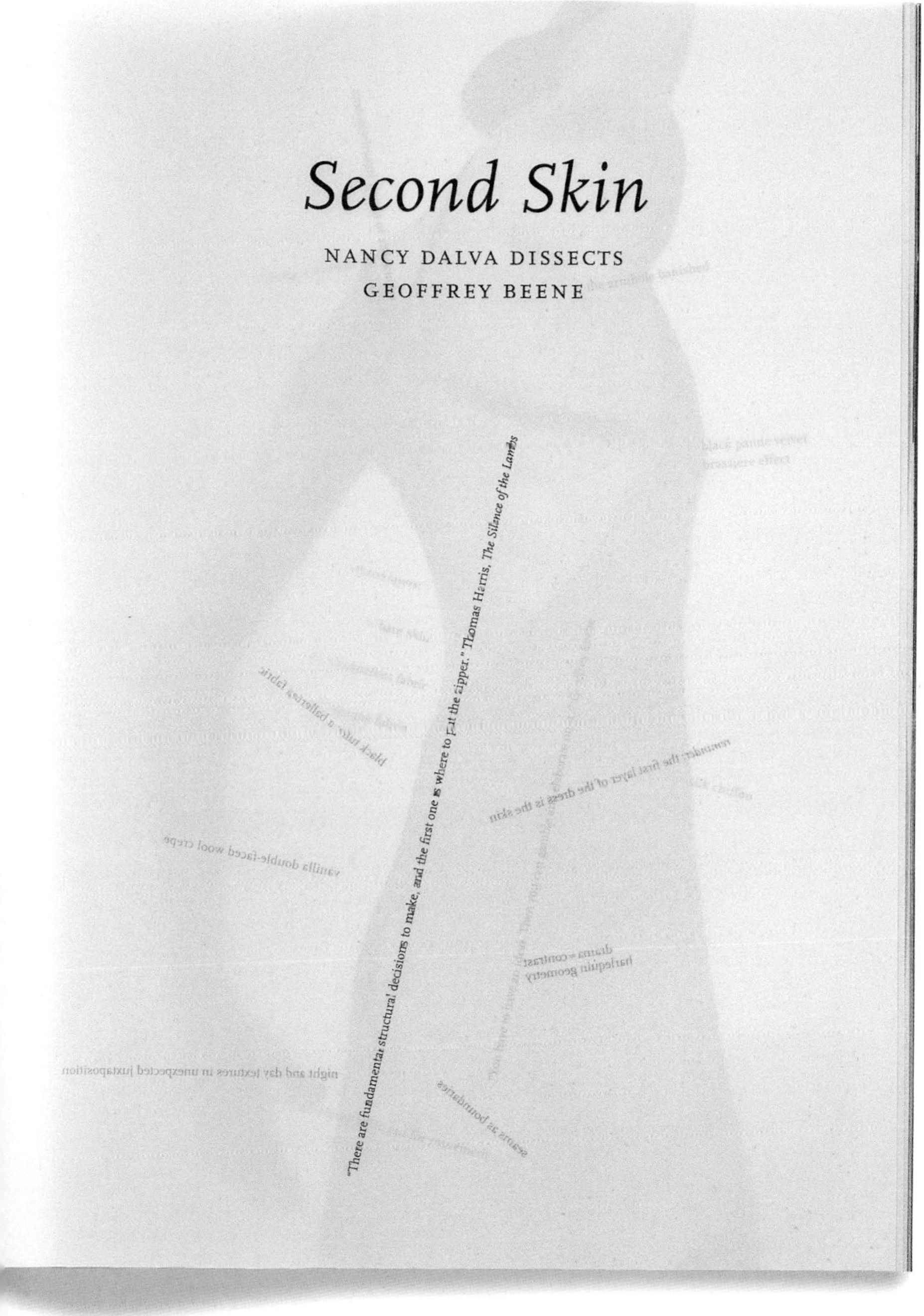

Second Skin

NANCY DALVA DISSECTS
GEOFFREY BEENE

DANCE INK: SECOND SKIN
Magazine, 1996
Designer: Abbott Miller
Photographer: Jack Deutsch
Publisher: Patsy Tarr
*Like a diagram from an
anatomy book, the typography
maps the body seen through
the skin of the page.*

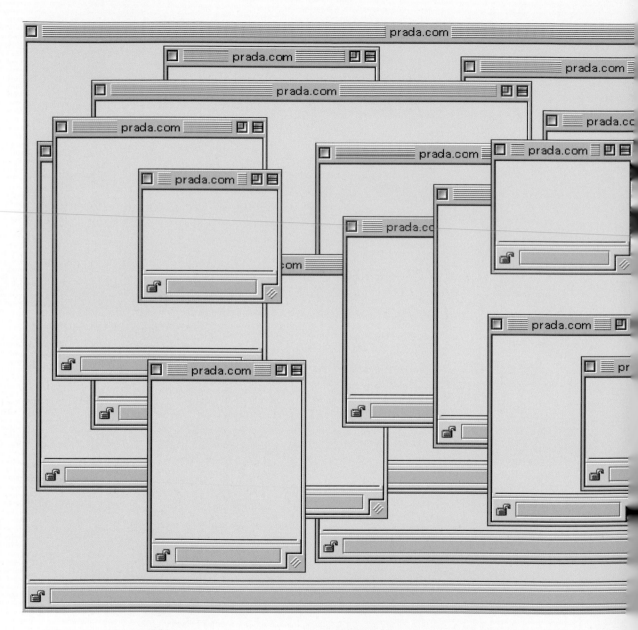

PRADA PROTOTYPE
Concept for Web site
Design: 2x4, New York

GRID

HISTORIA NATURALIS
Book, 1472; printed by
Nicolas Jenson, Venice
Collection of the Walters Art
Museum, Baltimore
*During the first century of
printing, the French-born
printer Nicolas Jenson
established a printing business
in Venice, a thriving commercial
center. This book features an
elegant, unbroken text block set
in one of the first roman
typefaces. The page has no line
breaks or indents.*

GRID

A GRID BREAKS SPACE OR TIME INTO REGULAR UNITS. A grid can be simple or complex, specific or generic, tightly defined or loosely interpreted. Typographic grids are all about control. They establish a system for arranging content within the space of page, screen, or built environment. Designed in response to the internal pressures of content (text, image, data) and the outer edge or frame (page, screen, window), an effective grid is not a rigid formula but a flexible and resilient structure, a skeleton that moves in concert with the muscular mass of information.

Grids belong to the technological framework of typography, from the concrete modularity of letterpress to the ubiquitous rulers, guides, and coordinate systems of graphics applications. Although software generates illusions of smooth curves and continuous tones, every digital image or mark is constructed—ultimately—from a grid of neatly bounded blocks. The ubiquitous language of the GUI (graphical user interface) creates a gridded space in which windows overlay windows in a haphazard way.

In addition to their place in the background of design production, grids have become explicit theoretical tools. Avant-garde designers in the 1910s and 1920s exposed the mechanical grid of letterpress, bringing it to the polemical surface of the page. In Switzerland after World War II, graphic designers built a total design methodology around the typographic grid, hoping to construct with it a new and rational social order.

The grid has evolved across centuries of typographic development. For graphic designers, grids are carefully honed intellectual devices, infused with ideology and ambition, and they are the inescapable mesh that filters, at some level of resolution, nearly every system of writing and reproduction.

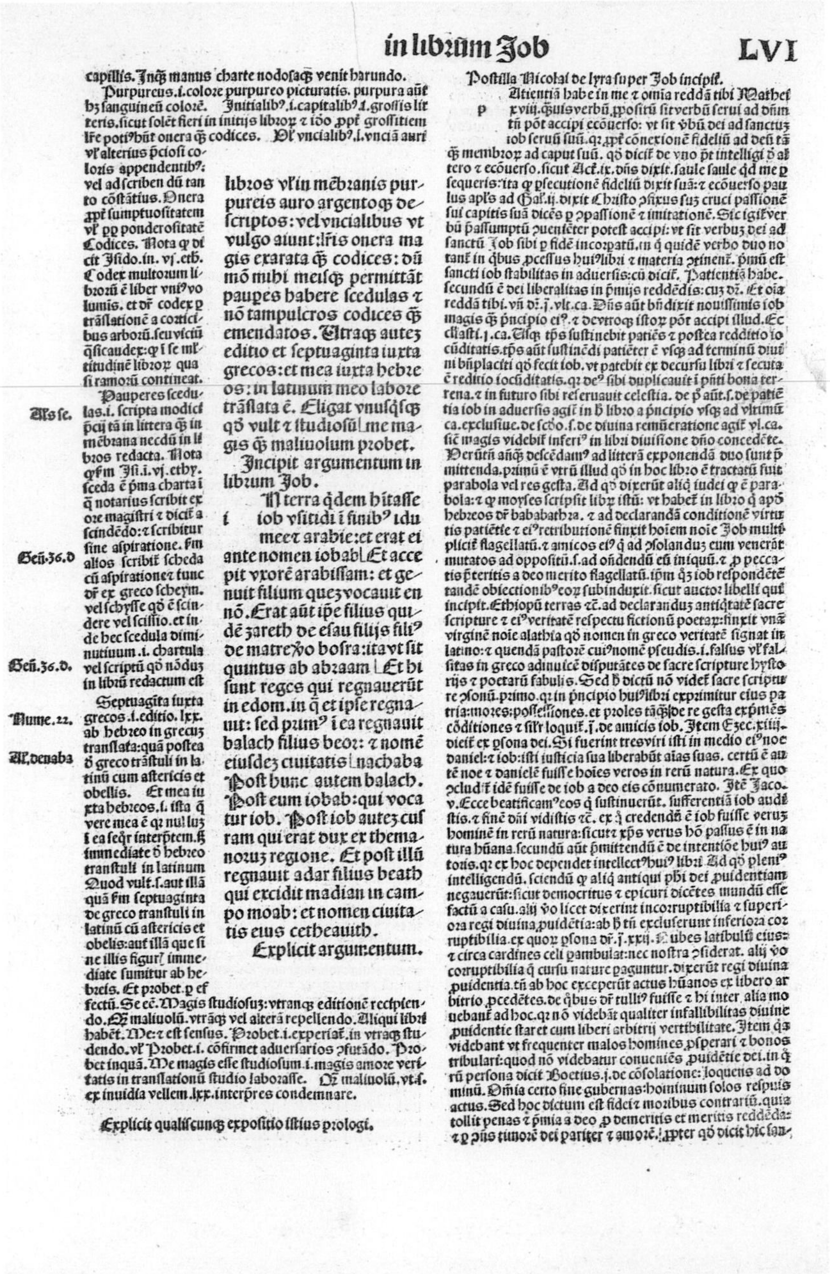
in librum Job LVI

libros vel in membranis purpureis auro argentoque descriptos: vel uncialibus ut vulgo aiunt: litteris onera magis exarata quam codices: dum mihi meisque permittant pauperes habere scedulas et non tam pulcros codices quam emendatos. Utraque autem editio et septuaginta iuxta grecos: et mea iuxta hebreos: in latinum meo labore translata est. Eligat unusquisque quod vult et studiosum me magis quam malivolum probet.

Incipit argumentum in librum Job.

In terra quidem habitasse iob ustidi in finibus idumee arabie: et erat ei ante nomen iobab. Et accepit uxorem arabissam: et genuit filium quem vocavit ennon. Erat autem ipse filius quidem zareth de esau filiis filius de matre vero bosra: ita ut sit quintus ab abraam. Et hi sunt reges qui regnaverunt in edom. in qua et ipse regnavit: sed primus in ea regnavit balach filius beor: et nomen eiusdem civitatis nachaba. Post hunc autem balach. Post eum iobab: qui vocatur iob. Post iob autem cusram qui erat dux ex themanorum regione. Et post illum regnavit adar filius beath qui excidit madian in campo moab: et nomen civitatis eius cetheauith.

Explicit argumentum.

LATIN BIBLE (LEFT)
Book page, 1497
Printed by
Anton Koberger

A two-column grid engulfs a second set of columns. Each page is a dense mass incised with narrow gutters and open spaces where illuminated capitals would have been added by hand. The layout changes from page to page.

GRID AS FRAME

Alphabetic writing, like most writing systems, is organized into columns and rows of characters. Whereas handwriting flows into connected lines, the mechanics of metal type impose a stricter order. Each letter occupies its own block, and the letters congregate in orderly rectangles. Stored in gridded cases, the characters become an archive of elements, a matrix of existing forms from which each page is composed.

Until the twentieth century, grids served as frames for fields of text. The margins of a classical book page create a pristine barrier around a flush, solid block of text. A page dominated by a solitary field of type remains today's most common book format, although that perfect rectangle is now broken with indents and line breaks, and the margins are peppered with page numbers and running heads (text indicating the book or chapter title).

In addition to the classical norm of the single-column page, various alternative layouts existed during the first centuries of printing, from the two-column grid of Gutenberg's Bible to more elaborate layouts derived from the medieval scribal tradition, where passages of scripture are surrounded by scholarly commentary. Polyglot (multilingual) books display a text in several languages simultaneously, demanding complex divisions of the surface.

Such formats permit multiple streams of text to coexist while defending the sovereignty of the page-as-frame. The philosopher Jacques Derrida has described the frame in Western art as a form that seems to be separate from the work yet is necessary for marking its difference from everyday life. A frame or pedestal elevates the work, removing it from the realm of the ordinary. The work thus depends on the frame for its status and visibility.

Typography is, by and large, an art of framing, a form designed to melt away as it yields itself to content. Designers focus much of their energy on margins, edges, and empty spaces, elements that oscillate between present and absent, visible and invisible. With print's ascent, margins became the user interface of the book, providing space for page numbers, running heads, commentary, notes, and ornaments.

The frame...disappears, buries itself, effaces itself, melts away at the moment it deploys its greatest energy. The frame is in no way a background...but neither is its thickness as margin a figure. Or at least it is a figure that comes away of its own accord. Jacques Derrida, 1987

CAPVT PRIMVM.

IN principio creauit Deus cælum & terrá. [2] Terra autem erat inanis & vacua: & tenebræ erant super faciê abyssi: & spiritus Dei ferebatur super aquas. [3] Dixitq́, Deus, Fiat lux. Et facta est lux. [4] Et vidit Deus lucem quòd esset bona:& diuisit lucem à tenebris. [5] Appellauitq́, lucem diem;& tenebras noctê. Factumq́; est vespere & mane dies vnus. [6] Dixit quoque Deus, Fiat firmamentû in medio aquarum; & diuidat aquas ab aquis. [7] Et fecit Deus firmamentum, diuisitq́; aquas quæ erant sub firmamento, ab his quæ erant super firmamentû. Et factum est ita. [8] Vocauitq́; Deus firmamentû, cælum: & factum est vespere, & mane dies secundus.

[9] Dixit verò Deus, Congregentur aquæ quæ sub cælo sunt, in locum vnum:& appareat arida.Et factum est ita. [10] Et vocauit Deus aridã, terram:congregationéq; aquarum appellauit maria. Et vidit Deus quòd esset bonum. [11] Et ait, Germinet terra herbã virentem & facientem semen; & lignum pomiferû faciens fructû iuxta genus suum, cuius semen in semetipso sit super terram.Et factû est ita. [12] Et protulit terra herbam virentê, & facientê semen iuxta genus suû; lignumq́; faciens fructû, & habens vnumquodq; sementem secundû speciem suam. Et vidit Deus quòd esset bonum. [13] Et factum est vespere & mane dies tertius. [14] Dixit autê Deus, Fiant luminaria in firmamento cæli; & diuidant diem ac noctê; & sint in signa & têpora & dies & annos; [15] Vt luceát in firmaméto cæli, & illuminent terrã.Et factum est ita. [16] Fecitq́; Deus duo luminaria magna: luminare maius, vt præesset diei: & luminare minus,vt præesset nocti: & stellas. [17] Et posuit eas Deus in firmaméto cæli, vt luceret super terrã: [18] Et præessent diei ac nocti;& diuiderent lucem ac tenebras. Et vidit Deus quòd esset bonû. [19] Et factum est vespere, & mane dies quartus. [20] Dixit etiam Deus,Producant aquæ reptile animæ viuentis, & volatile super terram sub firmamento cæli.

Hebrew text

בראשית ברא אלהים את השמים ואת הארץ: והארץ היתה תהו ובהו וחשך על פני תהום ורוח אלהים מרחפת על פני המים: ויאמר אלהים יהי אור ויהי אור: וירא אלהים את האור כי טוב ויבדל אלהים בין האור ובין החשך: ויקרא אלהים לאור יום ולחשך קרא לילה ויהי ערב ויהי בקר יום אחד:
ויאמר אלהים יהי רקיע בתוך המים ויהי מבדיל בין מים למים: ויעש אלהים את הרקיע ויבדל בין המים אשר מתחת לרקיע ובין המים אשר מעל לרקיע ויהי כן: ויקרא אלהים לרקיע שמים ויהי ערב ויהי בקר יום שני:
ויאמר אלהים יקוו המים מתחת השמים אל מקום אחד ותראה היבשה ויהי כן: ויקרא אלהים ליבשה ארץ ולמקוה המים קרא ימים וירא אלהים כי טוב: ויאמר אלהים תדשא הארץ דשא עשב מזריע זרע עץ פרי עשה פרי למינו אשר זרעו בו על הארץ ויהי כן: ותוצא הארץ דשא עשב מזריע זרע למינהו ועץ עשה פרי אשר זרעו בו למינהו וירא אלהים כי טוב: ויהי ערב ויהי בקר יום שלישי:
ויאמר אלהים יהי מארת ברקיע השמים להבדיל בין היום ובין הלילה והיו לאתת ולמועדים ולימים ושנים: והיו למאורת ברקיע השמים להאיר על הארץ ויהי כן: ויעש אלהים את שני המארת הגדלים את המאור הגדל לממשלת היום ואת המאור הקטן לממשלת הלילה ואת הכוכבים: ויתן אתם אלהים ברקיע השמים להאיר על הארץ: ולמשל ביום ובלילה ולהבדיל בין האור ובין החשך וירא אלהים כי טוב: ויהי ערב ויהי בקר יום רביעי:
ויאמר אלהים ישרצו המים שרץ נפש חיה ועוף יעופף על הארץ על פני רקיע השמים:

תרגום אונקלוס

בקדמין ברא יי ית שמיא וית ארעא: וארעא הות צדיא וריקניא וחשוכא על אפי תהומא ורוחא מן קדם יי מנשבא על אפי מיא: ואמר יי יהי נהורא והוה נהורא: וחזא יי ית נהורא ארי טב ואפריש יי בין נהורא ובין חשוכא: וקרא יי לנהורא יממא ולחשוכא קרא ליליא והוה רמש והוה צפר יומא חד: ואמר יי יהי רקיעא במציעות מיא ויהי מפריש בין מיא למיא: ועבד יי ית רקיעא ואפריש בין מיא דמלרע לרקיעא ובין מיא דמעל לרקיעא והוה כן: וקרא יי לרקיעא שמיא והוה רמש והוה צפר יום תנין: ואמר יי יתכנשון מיא מתחות שמיא לאתר חד ותתחזי יבשתא והוה כן: וקרא יי ליבשתא ארעא ולבית כנישות מיא קרא יממי וחזא יי ארי טב: ואמר יי תדאית ארעא דתאה עסבא דבר זרעיה מזדרע אילן פירין עבד פירין לזניה דבר זרעיה ביה על ארעא והוה כן: ואפיקת ארעא דתאה עסבא דבר זרעיה מזדרע לזנוהי ואילן עבד פירין דבר זרעיה ביה לזנוהי וחזא יי ארי טב: והוה רמש והוה צפר יום תליתאי: ואמר יי יהון נהורין ברקיעא דשמיא לאפרשא בין יממא ובין ליליא ויהון לאתין ולזמנין ולממני בהון יומין ושנין: ויהון לנהורין ברקיעא דשמיא לאנהרא על ארעא והוה כן: ועבד יי ית תרין נהוריא רברביא ית נהורא רבא למשלט ביממא וית נהורא זעירא למשלט בליליא וית כוכביא: ויהב יתהון יי ברקיעא דשמיא לאנהרא על ארעא: ולמשלט ביממא ובליליא ולאפרשא בין נהורא ובין חשוכא וחזא יי ארי טב: והוה רמש והוה צפר יום רביעאי:

CAPVT PRIMVM.

N principio fecit Deus cælum & terra.* At terra erat inuisibilis et incôposita, et tenebræ super abyssum: & spiritus Dei ferebatur super aquam. * Et dixit Deus, Fiat lux, & facta est lux. * Et vidit Deus lucê, quòd bona: & diuisit Deus inter lucem, & inter tenebras. * Et vocauit Deus lucê diê: & tenebras vocauit noctê: & factû est vespere, & factû est mane, dies vnus. * Et dixit Deus, Fiat firmamentû in medio aquæ: & sit diuidês inter aquâ, & aquâ.* Et fecit Deus firmamentû, & diuisit Deus inter aquâ, quæ erat sub firmamento: & inter aquâ, quæ super firmamentû. * Et vocauit Deus firmamentû cæli: & vidit Deus, quòd bonû. Et factû est vespere, & factû est mane, dies secudus. * Et dixit Deus, Côgregetur aqua quæ sub cælo, in cogregatione vnâ, & appareat arida. Et factû ita est. * Et cogregata est aqua quæ sub cælo, in cogregationes suas: & apparuit arida. * Et vocauit Deus aridâ, terrâ: et cogregationes aquarû, vocauit maria. Et vidit Deus quòd bonû. * Et dixit Deus, Germinet terra herbâ fœni semmantê semê secundû genus et secundû similitudinê: & lignû pomiferû faciens fructû, cuius semen ipsius in ipso secundû genus super terrâ. Et factum est ita. * Et protulit terra herbâ fœni semmantê semen secundû genus & secundû similitudinê: & lignû pomiferû faciens fructû, cuius semê eius in ipso, secundû genus super terrâ. Et vidit Deus quòd bonû. * Et factû est vespere, & factû est mane, dies tertius. * Et dixit Deus, Fiant luminaria in firmamento cæli, vt luceant super terrâ, ad diuidendum inter diê, & inter noctê: & sint in signa, & in tépora, & in dies, & in annos. * Et sint in illuminatione in firmamento cæli, vt luceant super terram. Et factû est ita. * Et fecit Deus duo luminaria magna: luminare magnû in principatus dici: & luminare minus, in principat noctis: et stellas. * Et posuit eas Deus in firmamêt cæli: vt lucerêt super terrâ, * Et præessent diei, & nocti, & diuiderent inter lucê et inter tenebras: et vidit Deus quòd bonû. * Et factû est vespere, & factû est mane, dies quartus. * Et dixit Deus, Producant aquæ reptilia animarû viuentiû, & volatilia volatia super terrâ, secundû firmamentû cæli: & factû est ita.

CHALDAICÆ PARAPHRASIS TRANSLATIO.
CAPVT PRIMVM.

IN principio creauit Deus cælum & terram.* Terra autem erat deserta & vacua; & tenebræ super faciem abyssi: & spiritus Dei insufflabat super faciem aquarum. * Et dixit Deus, Sit lux: & fuit lux. * Et vidit Deus lucem quòd esset bona. Et diuisit Deus inter lucem & inter tenebras. * Appellauitque Deus lucem diem, & tenebras vocauit noctem. Et fuit vespere & fuit mane dies vnus. * Et dixit Deus, Sit firmamentum in medio aquarum: & diuidat inter aquas & aquas. * Et fecit Deus firmamentum: & diuisit inter aquas quæ erant sub firmamento: & inter aquas quæ erant super firmamentum: & fuit ita. * Et vocauit Deus firmamentum cælum. Et fuit vespere & fuit mane, dies secundus. * Et dixit Deus, Congregentur aquæ quæ sub cælo sunt, in locum vnum: & appareat arida. Et fuit ita. * Et vocauit Deus aridam terram: & locum congregationis aquarum appellauit maria. Et vidit Deus quòd esset bonum. * Et dixit Deus, Germinet terra germinationem herbæ, cuius filius sementis seminatur: arboremque fructiferam facientem fructum secundum genus suum, cuius filius sementis in ipso super terram. Et fuit ita. * Et produxit terra germen herbæ, cuius filius sementis seminatur secundum genus suum; & arborem facientem fructû, cuius filius sementis in ipso secundum genus suum. Et vidit Deus quòd esset bonum. * Et fuit vespere & fuit mane, dies tertius. * Et dixit Deus, Sint luminaria in firmamento cæli, vt diuidant inter diem & noctem: & sint in signa & in tempora: & vt numerentur per eas dies & anni. * Et sint in luminaria in firmamento cæli ad illuminandum super terram: & fuit ita. * Et fecit Deus duo luminaria magna: luminare maius, vt dominaretur in die: & luminare minus, vt dominaretur in nocte: & stellas. * Et posuit eas Deus in firmamento cæli ad illuminandum super terram. * Et vt dominarentur in die & in nocte: & vt diuiderent inter lucê & tenebras: & vidit Deus quòd esset bonum. * Et fuit vespere & fuit mane, dies quartus. * Et dixit Deus, Serpant aquæ repule animæ viuentis: & auem quæ volat super terrâ super faciê aëris firmamenti cælorum.

A 2

348 SUPPLEMENT DE L'ANT. EXPLIQ. Liv. VI.

CHAPITRE SECOND.

I. La colonne de Pompée. II. On ne convient pas sur ses mesures. III. Colonne d'Alexandre Severe.

I. LA fameuse ² colonne de Pompée est auprès d'Alexandrie : on ne sait pour quelle raison elle porte le nom de Pompée ; je croirois volontiers que c'est par quelque erreur populaire. Plusieurs voiageurs en ont parlé, tous conviennent qu'elle est d'une grandeur énorme. Deux des plus modernes en ont donné le dessein & les mesures ; mais ils different considerablement entre eux sur la hauteur du piedestal, de la colonne & du chapiteau : cependant tous deux disent qu'ils l'ont mesurée.

„ Pour ce qui est de la colonne, dit l'un, (c'est Corneille Brun p. 241.)
„ elle est sur un piedestal quarré, haut de sept ou huit pieds & large de qua-
„ torze à chacune de ses faces. Ce piedestal est posé sur une base quarrée,
„ haute d'environ un demi pied, & large de vingt, faite de plusieurs pierres
„ maçonnées ensemble. Le corps de la colonne même n'est que d'une seule
„ pierre, que quelques-uns croient être de granit ; d'autres disent que c'est
„ une espece de pâte ou de ciment, qui avec le tems a pris la forme de pierre.
„ Pour moi je croi que c'est une vraie pierre de taille, du moins autant que
„ j'ai pu le reconnoitre par l'épreuve que j'en ai faite. Et si cela est vrai, com-
„ me personne presque n'en doute, il y a sujet de s'étonner comment on a
„ pu dresser une pierre de cette grandeur : car après l'avoir mesurée, j'ai trou-
„ vé qu'elle a quatre-vingt-dix pieds de haut, & que sa grosseur est telle, que
„ six hommes peuvent à peine l'embrasser ; ce qui revient, selon la mesure
„ que j'en ai prise, à trente-huit pieds. Au haut il y a un beau chapiteau pro-
„ portionné à la grosseur de la colonne, mais fait d'une piece separée.

L'autre, qui est M. Paul Lucas, en parle en cette maniere : „ Un de mes
„ premiers soins fut d'aller examiner la colonne de Pompée, qui est près d'A-
„ lexandrie du côté du couchant, & je croi qu'il seroit difficile de rien ajou-

---

CAPUT SECUNDUM.

I. Columna Pompeii, II. De ejus mensuris non convenit inter eos qui istæc loca adierunt. III. Columna Alexandri Severi.

I. CEleberrima ² illa Pompeii columna prope Alexandriam erigitur. Cur Pompeii columna vocetur, ignoratur. Libenter crederem hujusmodi denominationem ex populari errore manavisse. Ex peregrinantibus omnes enormis magnitudinis esse narrant. Duo recentiores & figuram & mensuras dederunt, at inter illos non convenit de stylobate, columnæ & capitelli magnitudine. Attamen ambo dicunt se mensuras excepisse.

„ Quantum ad columnam, inquit Cornelius
» Brunius p. 241. ea imposita est quadrato styloba-
» tæ cujus altitudo est septem octove pedum, la-
» tera vero singulis in faciebus sunt quatuordecim
» pedum. Stylobates autem ille quadratæ basi im-

» ponitur, altitudine dimidii pedis, ex lapidibus
» plurimis structa basis est, longitudinis circum-
» quaque viginti pedes habens. Columna ex uno
» lapide est, plurimi putant ex marmore granito
» esse, alii vero quasi cæmentum & compactam
» materiam esse, quæ procedente tempore, formam
» lapidis sumserit. Puto ego esse lapidem quantum
» saltem experiri licuit. Quod si ita sit, id autem
» nemo hodie in dubium vocat ; plane mirum
» quo pacto tantum lapidem erigere potuerint.
» Nam cum mensuram duxissem, nonaginta pedes
» altitudinis habere comperi, tantaque ejus est spis-
» situdo, ut sex viri simul vix illam amplecti pos-
» sint, id quod ad mensuram a me sumtam redu-
» citur, circuitus enim ejus est triginta & octo
» pedum. In culmine capitellum est ex uno lapide
» secundum columnæ proportionem.

Alius, nempe Paulus Lucas, columnam sic des-
cribit. » Ubi primum porui columnam Pompeii
» adii, quæ prope Alexandriam est versus oc-
» cidentem. Difficile autem esset ejus mensuras

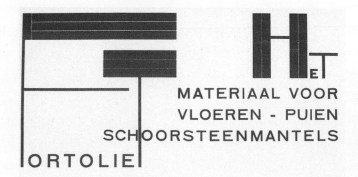

DIVIDING SPACE

In the nineteenth century, the multi-columned, multimedia pages of newspapers and magazines challenged the supremacy of the book and its insular edge, making way for new typogologies of the grid. By questioning the protective function of the frame, modern artists and designers unleashed the grid as a flexible, critical, and systematic tool. Avant-garde artists and poets attacked the barriers between art and everyday life, creating new objects and practices that merged with urban experience.

The assault against print's traditional syntax was led by F. T. Marinetti, who established the Futurist movement in 1909. Marinetti devised poems that combined different styles and sizes of type and allowed lines of text to span multiple rows. Marinetti's ingenius manipulations of the printing process work against—but inside—the constraints of letterpress, exposing the technological grid even while trying to overturn it. Dada artists and poets performed similar typographic experiments, using letterpress printing as well as collage, montage, and various forms of photomechanical reproduction.

Constructivism, which originated in the Soviet Union at the end of the 1910s, built on Futurist and Dada typography, bringing a more rational approach to the attack on typographic tradition. El Lissitzky employed the elements of the print shop to emphasize the mechanics of letterpress, using printer's rules to make the technological matrix actively and physically present. Constructivism used rules to divide space, throwing its symmetry into a new kind of balance. The page was no longer a fixed, hierarchical window through which content might be viewed, but an expanse that could be mapped and articulated, a space extending beyond the edge.

For Dutch artists and designers, the grid was a gateway to the infinite. The paintings of Piet Mondrian, their abstract surfaces crossed by vertical and horizontal lines, suggest the expansion of the grid beyond the limits of the canvas. Theo van Doesburg, Piet Zwart, and other members of the Dutch De Stijl group applied this idea to design and typography. Converting the curves and angles of the alphabet into perpindicular systems, they forced the letter through the mesh of the grid. Like the Constructivists, they used vertical and horizontal bars to structure the surface of the page.

Typography is mostly an act of dividing a limited surface. Willi Baumeister, 1923

die werkstätten befinden sich dessau seilerschefabrik eingang rennstr

der direktor

das bauhaus in dessau
dessau mauerstraße 36 ● fernruf 2696   städt. kreisspark. dessau 2634 ● postscheck magdeburg 13701

ihre zeichen   ihre nachricht vom   unsere zeichen   tag

betreff

bauhausdruck bayer

din a 4

versuch einer vereinfachten schreibweise: 1. diese schreibweise wird von allen neuerern der schrift als unsere zukunftschrift empfohlen. vergl. das buch „sprache und schrift" von dr. porstmann, verlag des vereins deutscher ingenieure, berlin 1920.   2. durch kleinschreibung verliert unsere schrift nichts, wird aber leichter lesbar, leichter lernbar, wesentlich wirtschaftlicher.   3. warum für einen laut, z. b. a zwei zeichen A und a ? ein laut ein zeichen. warum zwei alfabete für ein wort, warum die doppelte menge zeichen, wenn die hälfte dasselbe erreicht?

DAS BAUHAUS IN DESSAU
Letterhead, 1924
Designer: Herbert Bayer
Collection of Elaine Lustig
Cohen
*Herbert Bayer's letterheads for
the Bauhaus are manifestos for
a new typographic order. Rather
than provide a decorative frame
or a centered title, Bayer treated
the entire page as a surface to be
divided. Points, short hatches,
and lines of type indicate axes
for folding the sheet and
positioning text. This letterhead
also promotes Bayer's idea that
all letters should be lowercase,
a point expounded in small
print across the bottom.*

**The new typography not only contests the classical "framework"
but also the whole principle of symmetry.** Paul Renner, 1931

Jan Tschichold's book *The New Typography*, published in Germany in 1928, took ideas from Futurism, Constructivism, and De Stijl and conveyed them as practical advice for commercial printers and designers. Functionally zoned letterheads using standard paper sizes were central to Tschichold's practical application of modernism. Whereas Futurism and Dada had aggressively attacked convention, Tschichold advocated design as a means of discipline and order, and he began to theorize the grid as a modular system based on standard measures.

By describing the expansion of space in all directions, the modern grid slipped past the classical frame of the page. Similarly, modern architecture had displaced the centered facades of classical building with broken planes, modular elements, and continuous ribbons of windows.

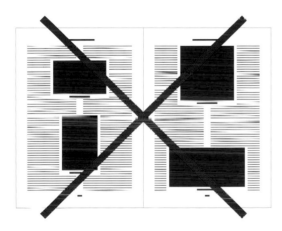 

THE NEW TYPOGRAPHY
Diagram, 1928
(redrawn)
Designer and author:
Jan Tschichold

Tschichold's diagram of good and bad magazine design advocates staggering images in relation to content instead of forcing text to wrap around blocks moored at the center of the page. Explaining this experiment, Tschichold wrote that his redesigned pages would be even more effective if the photographic halftones (called "blocks") were produced in fixed rather than arbitrary sizes.

I have intentionally shown blocks of different and "accidental" widths, since this is what usually has to be contended with (although in the future, with standard block-sizes, it will happen less often).
Jan Tschichold, 1928

ZAHN-NOPPER
Store identity, 1961–63
Designer: Jochen Stankowski
*This identity system
demonstrates a programmatic
approach to design, using a
limited set of elements to
construct diverse yet genetically
linked solutions. The system is
not grounded is governed by
flexible rules for construction
rather than a fixed logotype.*

GRID AS PROGRAM

Classics of Swiss design theory include Josef Müller-Brockmann, *Grid Systems in Graphic Design* (Switzerland: Ram Publications, 1996; first published in 1961) and *The Graphic Artist and his Design Problems* (Switzerland: Arthur Niggli Ltd., 1961); and Karl Gerstner, *Designing Programmes* (Switzerland: Arthur Niggli, 1964). See also Emil Ruder, *Typography* (New York: Hastings House, 1981, first published in 1967).

During the post–World War II period, graphic designers in Switzerland honed ideas from the New Typography into a total design methodology. It was at this time that the term "grid" (*raster*) became commonly applied to page layout. Max Bill, Karl Gerstner, Josef Müller-Brockmann, Emil Ruder, and others were practitioners and theorists of a new rationalism that aimed to catalyze an honest and democratic society. Rejecting the artistic clichés of self expression and raw intuition, they aspired to what Ruder called "a cool and fascinating beauty."

Karl Gerstner's book *Designing Programmes* (1964) is a manifesto for systems-oriented design. Gerstner defined a design "programme" as a set of rules for constructing a range of visual solutions. Connecting his methodology with the new field of computer programming, Gerstner presented examples of computer-generated patterns that were made by mathematically describing visual elements and combining them according to simple rules.

Expanding on the pioneering ideas of Bayer, Tschichold, Renner, and other designers of the avant garde, the Swiss rationalists rejected the centuries-old model of the page-as-frame in favor of a continuous architectural space. Whereas a traditional book would have placed captions, commentary, and folios within a protective margin, the rationalist grid cut the page into multiple columns, each bearing equal weight within the whole, suggesting an indefinite progression outward. Pictures were cropped to fit the modules of the grid, yielding shapes of unusual proportion. Constructing ever more elaborate grids, the Swiss designers used the confines of a repeated structure to generate variation and surprise. Such grids could be activated in numerous ways within a single publication, always referring back to the root structure.

This approach, which quickly became known as "Swiss design," found adherents (and detractors) around the world. Many American designers dismissed Swiss rationalism as irrelevant to a society driven by pop culture and hungry for rapidly transforming styles. Programmatic thinking is now being revived, however, as designers today confront large-scale information projects. The need is greater than ever for flexible "programs" accommodating dynamic bodies of content.

The typographic grid is a proportional regulator for composition, tables, pictures, etc....
The difficulty is: to find the balance, the maximum of conformity to a rule with the maximum
of freedom. Or: the maximum of constants with the greatest possible variability.
Karl Gerstner, 1961

14. Eingangshalle

15. Treppe

2 Mehrfamilienhäuser im Doldertal Zürich

Räumliche Organisation

Situation: Die beiden Mehrfamilienhäuser liegen im Villenviertel, auf halber Höhe des westwärts abfallenden „Zürichberg" [4]. Längs dem Grundstück verläuft auf der Nordwestseite eine öffentliche Parkanlage mit einem dichten Baumbestand. Die Zufahrtsstrasse genannt „Doldertal" hat ein Gefälle von 10 % und ist nicht durchgehend. Die Schrägstellung der Blöcke zur Baulinie ergibt eine verbesserte Südlage für die Wohnräume, eine Abdrehung der Schlafräume von der Strasse und eine lockere Gesamtanlage, ohne gegenüberliegende Schmalseiten. [5]   (Siehe auch baugesetzliche Sonderheiten.) Raumprogramm: Es ist versucht worden, die Vorzüge des Einfamilienhauses soweit als möglich auf die Etagenwohnung zu übertragen (freies, schallsicheres Wohnen, Einbeziehung der Landschaft, grosse Wohnterrassen, weitgehende innere Ausstattung). Im Untergeschoss: Gedeckter Vorplatz mit zwei Garagen, Eingangshalle mit Treppenaufgang, Abstellräume, Vorratskeller, Waschküche und Trockenraum, die beiden letzteren nur im untern Haus. Unter der Eingangshalle mit besonderem Eingang [9] [7] liegen Heizung und Kohlenraum. Im Parterre: eine Vierzimmerwohnung mit Mädchenzimmer und ein Einzimmer-Appartment mit direktem Eingang vom Garten. Im Obergeschoss: eine 5/6-Zimmerwohnung mit Mädchenzimmer. Zu dieser

Wohnung gehört noch ein auf Höhe Dachgeschoss liegendes Sonnenbad [12] [16], durch eine Eisentreppe von der Terrasse erreichbar. In beiden Wohnungen liegen Treppe und Küche ausserhalb der eigentlichen Wohnfläche (Schallisolation); dennoch hat die Küche eine betriebstechnisch zentrale Lage (Verbindung mit der Terrasse, je eine Durchreiche nach Essplatz und Treppenhaus). Im Dachgeschoss ein grosses und ein kleines Atelier, Abstellräume im Treppenbau.

Technische Durchbildung

(vgl. Technische Details)

Konstruktionsprinzip: Eisenskelett, Eisenbeton-Zwischendecken, Fassadenausmauerung mit gebrannten Hohlsteinen, hintermauert mit Gipsdielen. Die Fassaden sind konstruktiv von den Zwischendecken getrennt. Das zurückgesetzte Dachgeschoss besteht aus Holz mit einer äussern Eternitverkleidung. Zur Fertigstellung des Aussern sind ausschliesslich Materialien mit unterhaltsloser Oberfläche verwendet worden: Edelputz (weisser Zement, Natursteinpartikeln, ohne Farbgabe); Eternit für Rolladenkasten, Brüstungen, Sonnen-Storen-Vordach und Dachgeschossaufbau; lackiertes Holz für Rolladen und Garagentore; Kupfer für sämtliche Spenglerarbeiten; feuerverzinktes Eisen für Fensterbleche, Geländer. Gestrichen sind lediglich die Fenster und gewisse Metallteile aus architektonischen Gründen. Fensterflächen: Horizontal-Schiebefenster in Föhrenholz in den Woh-

nungen. Grösse des Normalfensters 310 × 120 cm, zusammengebaut mit dem Rolladenkasten; fester Teil einwärts klappbar zum Reinigen. Die Südfenster des Wohnraumes sind mit der Brüstung zusammengebaut (vgl. [21], [22], [23]). Die Küchenfenster sind doppelt, alle übrigen Fenster am Bau sind einfach verglast. Die Ateliers haben durchgehende 45 cm hohe Oberlichter unter der Decke mit Lüftungsklappen, sowie gewisse fest verglaste Fenster mit normaler Brüstung. Verglasung: Wohnungsfenster Spiegelglas 6/7 mm, Atelier-Oberlichter Rohglas, Treppenhausfenster Drahtglas. Sonnenschutz: für die Wohnzimmerfenster vor die Fassade gehängte Sonnenstoren [21] (44), für die Schlafzimmer Roll-Jalousien. Heizung: Jedes Haus hat seine eigene Warmwasserheizung für Kleinkaliberkoks, die gleichzeitig für die Warmwasserbereitung benützt wird. Pro Haus ein Warmwasserboiler mit 1000 Liter Inhalt.

Wohnungsausstattung: Die beiden Häuser sind für anspruchsvolle Mieter, jedoch ohne Luxus ausgestattet. Die Zimmer sind dementsprechend geräumig dimensioniert (Wohnraum 35,00 m², Terrasse 20,00 m²). Die Skelettkonstruktion erlaubt jederzeit eine den Wünschen der Mieter entsprechende Variabilität des Grundrisses. Im Wohnraum befindet sich ein offener Kamin und ein breites Fensterbrett für Blumen. Eingebaute Schränke im Korridor, in den Zimmern, kleiner Abstellraum. Fussböden: In den Wohnungen Holzmosaik (Esche im Wohnraum, Eiche in den übrigen Räumen und im Korridor).

2 Mehrfamilienhäuser im Doldertal Zürich   52

16. Teilansicht von Südwest mit Eingang und Garagen

In den Küchen sind Steinzeugplatten, versuchsweise Linoleum; in den Bädern Terrazzo, schwarz, mit weissen Marmorkörnern. Die Treppentritte und Podeste bestehen ebenfalls aus Terrazzo (Tritte fertige Platten, Podeste im Bau gegossen und geschliffen). Die Stirnseiten der Tritte und die Sockel sind mit weissen, hartglasierten Platten belegt [14]. Die Böden der Ateliers sind mit hellgrauem Linoleum belegt. Wandbehandlung: Gipsverputz in sämtlichen Räumen, Kalkabrieb in Küchen, Bädern und Aborten. Die Wände der Zimmer sind mit Leimfarbe gestrichen, mit Ausnahme derjenigen in den Wohnräumen und Gängen (tapeziert mit Grundpapier und Leimfarbanstrich, oder Ölfarbanstrich auf Stoffbespannung). In den Ateliers Verkleidung der Wände in Holzkonstruktion mit Sperrplatten (gewachste finnische Birke).
Im Treppenhaus: Aussenwand stoffbespannt, mit Ölfarbe gestrichen, mittlere Brüstungswand gespachtelt und Hochglanz mit Ripolin gestrichen; der Handlauf in Eisen, im Feuer weiss emailliert. Fenstersimsen: Diese bestehen in allen Räumen der Wohnungen aus perforierten, 3 cm starken Schieferplatten. Ausstattung der Bäder und Küchen: Grösse des Bades in den Wohnungen 6 m² mit Badwanne, Bidet und zwei Lavabos, W.C. Der Spiegel über den Lavabos ist gegen die festverglaste Fensterfläche gehängt (Licht auf das Gesicht). Die Küchen sind vollständig ausgestattet, je eine Durchreiche ins Treppenhaus und in den Wohn-Essraum, zweiteiliger Aufwaschtisch in Chrom-

nickel-Stahlblech, Kühlschrank, Arbeitsflächen in Ahornholz. Elektrische Beleuchtung: Diese ist in allen Wohn- und Schlafräumen, Gängen, Küchen, Ateliers eine indirekte.

Ökonomische Angaben
Die beiden Häuser sind Privatbesitz von Herrn Dr. S. Giedion, Zentralsekretär der Internationalen Kongresse für Neues Bauen. Die Baukosten inkl. Architektenhonorar betragen: 43,5 Maurerstunden pro m³ umbauten Raumes bei total 1985 m³ pro Haus, offene Halle im Parterre zur Hälfte gerechnet. Die durchschnittlichen Baukosten für normale Wohnbauten in Zürich, ohne besonderen Ausbau, betragen 38 bis 40 Maurerstunden pro m³ umbauten Raumes. (1 Mstd. = Fr. 1.72 1935/36)

Ästhetischer Aufbau
Die Schrägstellung der Blöcke ergibt einerseits eine lockere Gesamtanlage und erhöht anderseits deren plastische Selbständigkeit. Der zweigeschossige Charakter der Häuser (Baubestimmung der betreffenden Zone) wird durch das Loslösen des Baukörpers vom Terrain und durch das Zurücksetzen des Dachgeschosses gewahrt. Dieser Eindruck wird verstärkt durch die vom Hauptbau abweichende Konstruktion des Dachgeschosses (Holz und Eternit). In der Südfassade ist durch Weglassen der gemauerten Brüstungen ein äusseres Zusam-

menfassen von Wohnraum und Wohnterrasse erreicht. In der räumlichen Gliederung treten vielfach schräg verlaufende Wände auf, wodurch eine gewisse Auflockerung der Rechtwinkligkeit erreicht wird. Die Eingangshalle ganz in Glas hat eine freie Form und lässt den Durchblick in den rückwärtsliegenden Park frei.
Der Garten reicht über die weitergeführten Gartenplatten (Granit) bis zum Treppenaufgang. In den Wohnräumen und Ateliers reichen die Fenster bis zur Decke, in den Schlafräumen ist ein Sturz von 40 cm. In der Dimensionierung von Bauteilen und Ausstattungsdetails ist eine dem betreffenden Material entsprechende Sparsamkeit sowie eine organische und gepflegte Formgebung beobachtet worden. Materialbehandlung und Farbgebung: Aussen wirken die Baustoffe in ihrer natürlichen Struktur und Farbe: Edelputz, weisser Zement mit roten, schwarzen und glimmernden Steinsplittern, Eternit, lackiertes Holz, Eisenteile feuerverzinkt, mit Aluminiumfarbe gestrichen. Farbe an folgenden Stellen: Fensterrahmen dunkelgrau, Geländerrohre, Abdeckbleche weissgrau, die sichtbaren Kellermauern und Säulen sind normal verputzt und hellgrau gestrichen. Im Innern: Die Wände im Treppenhaus, in den Gängen und Nebenräumen sind weissgrau, ebenso das gesamte Holzwerk, Radiatoren, Leitungen. Die Wände der Wohn- und Schlafräume sind hell getönt (beige, rosa, hellblau, grau). Besondere farbige Akzente kommen weder aussen noch innen vor; es ist damit der wechselnden Bewohnung des Miethauses Rechnung getragen worden.

53   2 Mehrfamilienhäuser im Doldertal Zürich

DIE NEUE ARCHITEKTUR/
THE NEW ARCHITECTURE
Book, 1940
Designer: Max Bill
Author: Max Roth
Photograph: Dan Meyers

Designed by Max Bill in 1940, this book is considered the first use of a systematic, modular grid. Each image is sized to fit the column structure—as Jan Tschichold had predicted in 1928—filling one, two, or three zones. Acknowledging the originality of its layout, the author credits Bill as "the creator of the typographical structure of the book."

Der New-York-Times-Prospekt zeigt die Lösung einer komplexen Aufgabe; zeigt, wie eine Idee, ein Text und die typographische Darstellung über mehrere Phasen hinweg integriert werden. Darüber hinaus kann sich die Aufgabe stellen, Prospekte wie diesen wiederum mit andern Werbemitteln und Drucksachen zu integrieren. Denn heute brauchen Firmen mehr und mehr nicht bloss hier einen Prospekt, da ein Plakat, dort Inserate usw. Heute braucht eine Firma etwas anderes: Eine Physiognomie, ein optisches Gesicht.

Die Beispiele dieser Seiten geben die Physiognomie der boîte à musique, eines Grammophongeschäfts in Basel, wieder. Die boîte à musique hat ein Signet und einen firmeneigenen Stil – und doch wieder nicht, wenn man unter dem einen ein starres, nachträglich überall dazugesetztes Zeichen und unter dem andern ein bloss ästhetisches Prinzip versteht. Vielmehr: Die einmal definitiv festgelegten, aber jeweils den verschiedenen Funktionen und Proportionen angepassten Elemente selber bilden das Signum und den Stil in einem.

Abbildung 13 zeigt die Struktur. Fixiert sind die Elemente Schrift und Rahmen; ferner die Verbindung von beiden und das Prinzip der Variabilität: der Rahmen kann, ausgehend von der Ecke unten rechts, nach oben sowie nach links beliebig um ganze Einheiten vergrössert werden. Einen in sich proportional hervorragenden Fall gibt es nicht. Es gibt nur wertgleiche Varianten; und hervorragend ist die Variante dann, wenn sie der jeweiligen Aufgabe am besten angemessen ist.

Abbildung 14 zeigt die Neujahrskarte mit gleichzeitig verschieden proportionierten Varianten; 15 den Briefbogen, wo das Signum dem (gegebenen) Din A4 Format angepasst ist; 16 und 17 Inserate, wieder entsprechend dem zur Verfügung stehenden Insertionsraum bemessen; 18 ein Geschenkbon.

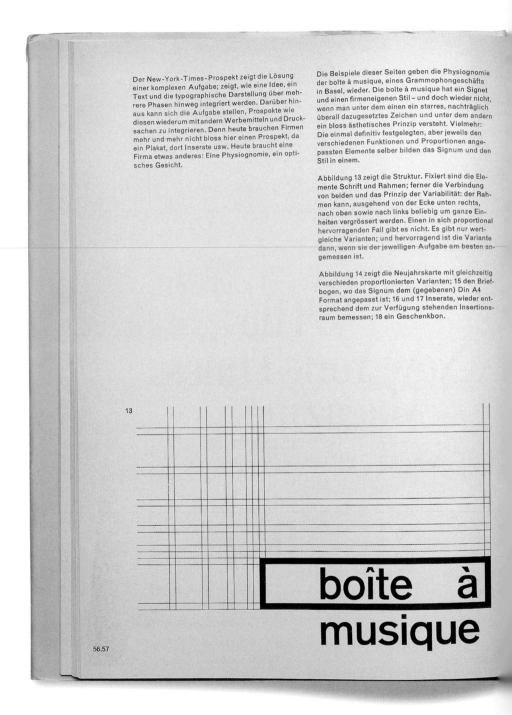

13

56.57

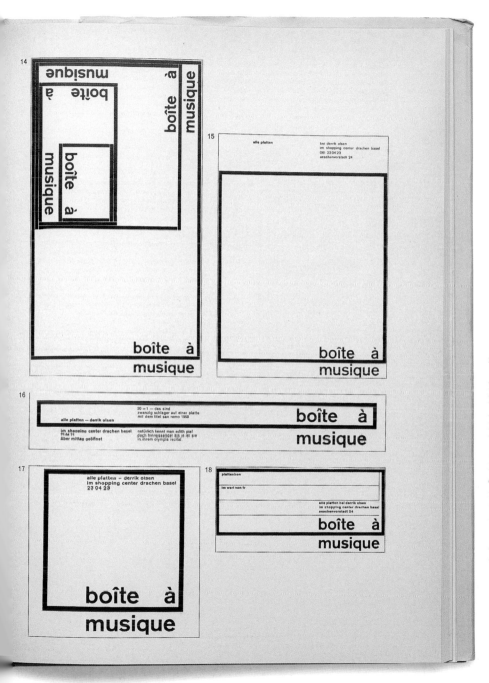

PROGRAMME ENTWERFEN
(DESIGNING PROGRAMS)
Book, 1964
Designer and author:
Karl Gerstner
Publisher: Arthur Niggli
Photograph: Dan Meyers
Karl Gerstner's book Designing
Programs *is a design theory
classic whose relevance has been
renewed in the age of networked
media. Shown here is Gerstner's
identity for Boîte à Musique
(Music Box), in which a system
of elements changes in response
to its context.*

GRID AS TABLE

Tables and graphs are a variant of the typographic grid. A table consists of vertical columns and horizontal rows, each cell occupied by data. A graph is a line mapped along the *x* and *y* axes of a grid, each dimension representing a variable (such as time and stock value, shown below). As explained by Edward Tufte, the leading critic and theorist of information design, tables and graphs allow relationships among numbers to be perceived and rapidly compared by the eye. In tables and graphs, the grid is a cognitive tool.

Tables are a central aspect of Web design. The table feature was incorporated into HTML code in 1995 so that Web authors could present tabular data. Graphic designers, eager to give shape to the Web's wide and flacid text bodies, quickly devised unauthorized uses for the HTML table, transforming this tool for representing data into nothing more nor less than a typographic grid. Designers have used the table feature to control the placement of images and captions and to build margins, gutters, and multicolumn screens. Designers also use tables to combine multiple styles of alignment—such as flush left and flush right—within a document, and to construct elegantly numbered and bulleted lists.

COLLAPSE OF ENRON (BELOW)
Interactive information graphic, 2002
NYTimes.com; courtesy of The New York Times
This on-line data graphic links a timeline of events leading to the financial collapse of the Enron Corporation with a graph of the company's stock price. As the user's cursor passes over each red circled number, text appears describing an event that occurred at that time. For example, in October the company's CEO froze his employees' 401(k) retirement funds as the company's stock was plummeting.

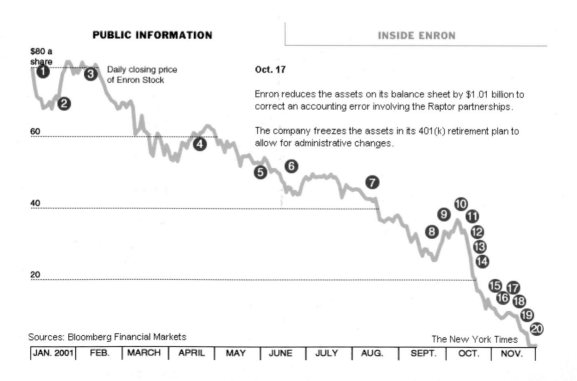

PUBLIC INFORMATION

INSIDE ENRON

Daily closing price of Enron Stock

Oct. 17

Enron reduces the assets on its balance sheet by $1.01 billion to correct an accounting error involving the Raptor partnerships.

The company freezes the assets in its 401(k) retirement plan to allow for administrative changes.

Sources: Bloomberg Financial Markets

The New York Times

| JAN. 2001 | FEB. | MARCH | APRIL | MAY | JUNE | JULY | AUG. | SEPT. | OCT. | NOV. |

On the aesthetics and ethics of information design, see Edward Tufte, *Envisioning Information* (Cheshire, Conn.: Graphics Press, 1990).

On designing accessible Web sites, see Patrick Lynch and Sarah Horton, *Web Style Guide: Basic Design Principles for Creating Web Sites* (New Haven: Yale University Press, 2001). See also the site www.webstyleguide.com.

By creating cells that span multiple columns and rows, designers build layout structures that bear little relation to the logically ordered fields of a data chart. A master table typically establishes areas for navigation, content, and site identity, and each region contains a smaller table—or tables—inside itself. Grids propagate inside of grids.

HTML purists reject such workarounds as spurious, even unethical, design tactics. Visually driven, illogical layout tables can cause problems for sight-impaired users, who implement various devices to translate digital pages into sound, cell by cell, row by row. Assistive screen readers "linearize" digital text into a stream of spoken words. Accessibility experts encourage Web designers to "think in linear terms" wherever possible, and to make sure their tables make sense when read in a continuous sequence. Accessible Web sites also consider the needs of users working with older software or text-only browsers. Linear thinking helps not only non-sighted audiences but also the users of cell phones, hand-held digital appliances, and other devices where space is tight and text is dominant.

MICA.EDU
Web site, 2004
Designers: Carton Donofrio Partners
Publisher: Maryland Institute College of Art
HTML tables, with their borders gently expressed, are an element of this neatly gridded Web page.

BEYOND HTML

HTML, the technology that allowed the Internet to become a global mass medium, is the virtual counterpart to letterpress, which mechanized the production of the book and cleared the ground for a world culture of print. Like letterpress, HTML is a text-hungry medium that can be coaxed, with some resistance, to display images. It is fundamentally driven by text, from its open, readable source code to the type of content it is designed to display.

HTML coexists with other languages on the Web, just as alternative technologies appeared alongside letterpress. Lithography, invented for the manufacture of images in the eighteenth century, quickly became an advertising medium that incorporated words as well as pictures, just as letterpress made space in its mechanical grid for woodcuts, engravings, and photographic halftone blocks. In the twentieth century, lithography replaced letterpress as the world's dominant printing method; used with digital or photographic typesetting, it conveys text and pictures with equal comfort.

Lithography is not governed by grids as relentlessly as letterpress; neither is Macromedia Flash, the animation software that became a common Web-design tool. Flash was originally designed for the creation of vector-based cartoons. Although its primary purpose was pictorial, it is now used to construct the interface and content, both graphic and textual, of entire Web sites.

Although Flash scripting manipulates objects in a field of *x* and *y* coordinates, the sites created with this technology often appear less tightly controlled by grids than the tabulated pages of HTML. The Flash sites that became, in the late 1990s, icons of a new Web aesthetic are more cinematic than typographic, and often feature a painterly mix of word and image.

Hand-coding HTML is as slow and deliberate as setting metal type. Empty table cells are used to out areas of open space, but HTML makes these collapse if the cells are truly empty, causing the grid to implode. The transparent images that often fill these spaces are virtual equivalents to the blank spacing material of metal type.

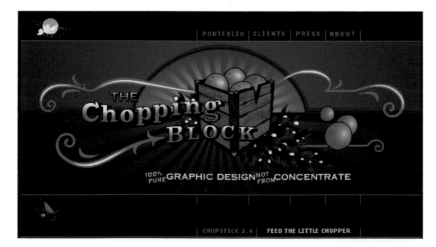

THE CHOPPING BLOCK
Web page (detail)
Designers: Thomas Romer, Jason Hillyer, Charles Michelet, Robert Reed, and Matthew Richmond, The Chopping Block
This Web site reprises the design of early twentieth-century fruit-crate labels, which were produced as lithographic prints that merge text and image. The Web page is animated, loading elements over time.

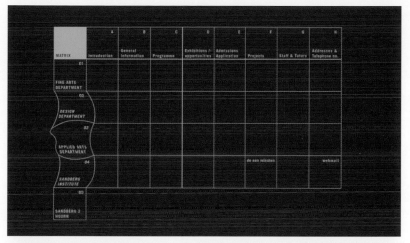

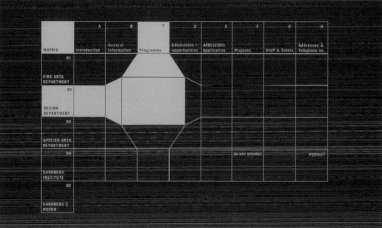

WWW.SANDBERG.NL
Web site, 2003
Designer: Luna Maurer
Publisher: Sandberg Institute
The grid is a navigation device that warps and changes as the user rolls over it. The vertical axis represents departments in the school, and the horizontal axis represents types of program information. As the user passes over the grid, cells fill with light and appear to lift away from the screen, indicating the availability of information at that intersection.

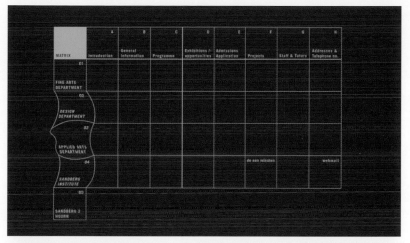

WILLIAM GIBSON'S 1984 NOVEL *Neuromancer* envisions cyberspace as a vast ethereal grid. Gibson's data cowboy leaves behind the "meat" of his body and drifts off into a "transparent 3D chessboard extending to infinity." The image of this grid is projected on an internal surface of the mind, bound by no screen or window.

The grid as infinite space—defying edges and dominated by mind rather than body—is a powerful instrument within modernist theory, where it is a form both rational and sublime. In the early twentieth century, avant-garde designers exposed the grid in order to dramatize the mechanical conditions of print. After World War II, Swiss designers built a total design methodology around the grid, infusing it with ideological intention. The grid was their key to a universal language. With the postmodern turn toward historical, vernacular, and popular sources in the 1970s and 1980s, many designers rejected the rationalist grid as a quaint artifact of Switzerland's own orderly society.

The rise of the Internet has rekindled interest in universal design thinking. The Web was invented in the early 1990s (in Switzerland) to let scientists and researchers share documents created with different software applications. Its inventor, Tim Berners-Lee, never guessed it would become a design-driven medium connecting vast numbers of differently abled and divergently motivated people around the globe.

Universal design systems can no longer be dismissed as the irrelevant musings of a small, localized design community. A second modernism has emerged, reinvigorating the utopian search for universal forms that marked the birth of design as a discourse and a discipline nearly a century earlier. Against the opacity and singularity of unique visual expressions—grounded in regional preferences and private obsessions— ideas of commonality, transparency, and openness are being reborn as information seeks to shed its physical body.

On the invention of the Web, see Tim Berners-Lee, *Weaving the Web* (New York: HarperCollins, 1999). For a contemporary account of universal design thinking, see William Lidwell, Kritina Holden, and Jill Butler, *Universal Principles of Design* (Gloucester, Mass.: Rockport Publishers, 2003). See also William Gibson, *Neuromancer* (New York: Ace Books, 1984).

To produce designs that are objectively informative is primarily a socio-cultural task. Josef Müller-Brockmann, 1961

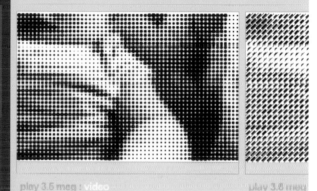

JOSHUADAVIS.COM
Web site, 2004
Designed by Joshua Davis
The anonymous coolness of "old school" Swiss rationalism resurfaced in Web design, as seen in the use of flush left, lowercase Helvetica and consistent grid systems.

Flash guru Joshua Davis, who designs serene screen layouts with scripted animations, is a leader in this return to the rational roots of mid-century graphics, now inflected with the voice of new media.

wild wirkende, dem Lennéschen Ideal folgende, baumreiche Naturgarten weicht englischen Rasenflächen, die sich mit nur noch wenigen Baum- und Strauchgruppen und gepflegten Blumenbeeten abwechseln. Mit dieser Veränderung, so der dritte Direktor des Zoos, Heinrich Bodinus, soll es möglich werden, den belebenden und erwärmenden Strahlen der Sonne Zutritt zu verschaffen. Anders als zuvor finden sich in den Berliner Zeitungen nun immer häufiger positiv gefärbte Erlebnisberichte. Vorläufiger Höhepunkt und nicht zu unterschätzender rite de passage für die breite Anerkennung des Gartens war das DREI-KAISER-TREFFEN im Herbst 1872: Kaiser Wilhelm, Kaiser Alexander II. von Rußland und Kaiser Franz-Joseph von Österreich-Ungarn werden in einem zwanzig Wagen umfassenden Zug über das Zoogelände kutschiert. Obwohl der Zoo zu dieser Zeit noch außerhalb der Stadt gelegen ist, ist dessen neuartige Gestaltung schon ein Zeichen dafür, daß die preußische Hauptstadt um die Anbindung an die Kultur der großen europäischen Metropolen bemüht ist. Die Bevölkerungszahl Berlins steigt mit der industriellen Entwicklung jener Jahre erheblich, und dem Zoo kommt (neben den Stadtparks) zunehmend ein Erholungswert zu, der durch eine Reihe von technischen Neuerungen gesteigert werden kann: eine Dampfmaschine sorgt für Wasserzirkulation und verwandelt die früher im Sommer übelriechenden Gewässer des Gartens in belebte Weiher. Hinzu kommt die Erleichterung von An- und Abreise. Ab 1875 verbindet eine Pferdebahnlinie Berlin mit dem Zoo. Im Jahre 1884 folgt die Installation elektrischer Beleuchtung, die eine Ausdehnung der Öffnungszeiten bis in die Abendstunden zuläßt. Kinderspielhallen und -plätze werden eingerichtet. Wo sonst könnten sie sicher vor dem Getümmel der Weltstadt in frischer Luft ihre Glieder üben und ihre Lungen weiten? heißt es im Programmheft des Jahres 1899. ‖ Der Zoo entwickelt sich deutlich zu einem integralen Bestandteil der städtischen Kultur. Anders als in den Stadtparks — etwa dem Humboldthain — stellt hier der Eintrittspreis sicher, daß das Vergnügen schmälernden Obdachlosen und Bettler vor den Toren bleiben. Zoofreunde werben um die Gunst von Kolonialoffizieren, die helfen sollen, die Tierbestände zu erhöhen und die in der Folge tatsächlich zunehmend als Donatoren fungieren. Forschungsreisen und Expeditionen in viele Regionen der Erde — häufig unter maßgeblicher Regie der Zoodirektoren — führen zur Entdeckung bislang unbekannter Tierarten. Die intensive Kooperation von Zoo und Naturkundemuseum setzt sich fort, so daß der Bestand des Museums 1894 auf etwa 2 Mio. Tiere, darunter etwa 150 000 Wirbeltiere, angewachsen ist. ‖ Der Berliner Zoo wird in den letzten Jahrzehnten des 19. Jahrhunderts zu einem repräsentativen Treffpunkt und zu einem Raum, in dem sich preußische Mentalität wenn auch nicht aufhebt, so doch aktiviert. Fremdartige Tierwelt und eine Architektur des Orient, des Fernen Osten und der Savannen, verbindet sich, in einiger Entfernung vom hektischen und geschäftigen Leben der Stadt, zu einem den Stadtbewohnern bis dahin unbekannten Ambiente. Hier entwickelt sich Natur zum Unterhaltungsgegenstand. Die von Zirkussen, Menagerien und Märkten bekannten sensationellen und theatralischen Aspekte gehen mit dem zoologischen Erkenntnisinteresse eine eigenartige Symbiose ein. Getragen wird diese Entwicklung nicht zuletzt

90 von ökonomischen Zwängen: immer wieder

kämpft die Zoogesellschaft um ihre Existenz. ‖ Der Zoo wird zu einem der Plätze der Stadt, wo sich Vorahnungen einer noch in Entwicklung begriffenen Weltstadt am ehesten materialisieren; kein Wunder, daß immer deutlicher auch Künstler und Gelehrte sich von diesem Raum angezogen fühlen. Neben einer Musiktribüne hilft ein erweiterter Restaurationsbetrieb den Aufenthalt in den meist nur unzureichend belüfteten Gebäuden aufzulockern. Ein Zeitgenosse beschreibt diese Bereicherung: Durch das neue Restaurationslokal ist die Zahl der großen Festsäle um ein Meisterwerk der Baukunst vermehrt worden. Wenn hier eine vortreffliche Militärkapelle ein Concert ausführt, dann bildet, in Folge des erhöhten Eintrittspreises, die elegante Welt die Mehrzahl der Besucher. Draußen dehnt sich eine lange Reihe Equipagen bis in die Winkel des Thiergartens; drinnen sind alle Plätze im weiten Umkreise des muschelförmig gebauten Orchesters besetzt; beim Klange der Instrumente, beim Geplätscher der Fontänen sitzt man, sich erfrischend, rauchend, plaudernd und scherzend unter den schattigen Bäumen und blickt in das abwechselnde, stets rege Thierleben hinaus, wie es sich in den benachbarten Grotten, auf Aesten und Teichen kund giebt.³ ‖ Die Auswahl der Tiere und der Situationen, in denen sich ihre Präsentation bewegte, erfolgt sorgfältig und bedacht, die Kuratoren entscheiden sich für besonders exotisch wirkende, kuriose, lächerliche, gefährliche Tiere.⁴ Dabei gilt es stets, die Konfrontation mit potentiell Abscheu oder starkes Befremden erregendem tierischem Verhalten zu verhindern. ‖ Die zunehmende Popularität der Zoos korreliert mit dem Verschwinden von Tieren aus dem Alltagsleben des städtischen Menschen. Das Tier ist entweder Haustier, also Mitbewohner der Wohnung, oder drastisch auf seine Rohstofffunktion reduziert und fristet in fabrikartigen Hallen abseits der Städte sein ökonomisch optimiertes Dasein. Mit den zoologischen Gärten beginnt ein Verdrängungsmechanismus, der sich später auch auf Naturparks und Reservate erstreckt: die Gefangenschaft erscheint angesichts der systematischen Zerstörung der Lebensräume als ein Schutz der Natur und dient dazu, das unterschwellig vorhandene schlechte Gewissen zu beruhigen.

(5) R. Springer: *Berlin: Die deutsche Kaiserstadt.* Reprint. Berlin 1877.
(6) Interessanterweise verbindet sich in einigen nordamerikanischen Gärten heute eine dem entgegengesetzte Entwicklung: Sowohl in Washington D.C. als auch in Montreal wurden ganze, unmaßstäblich weiträumige Tiere eingeführt, die immerhin 14 Procent des gesamten tierischen Lebens auf der Erde ausmachen. Diese Veränderung ist Teil einer Vielzahl von Eingriffen in die traditionelle Gestaltung, um einem grundlegend veränderten Verständnis von Mensch und Tierwelt Rechnung zu tragen. Vgl. Alexander Wilson: *The Culture of Nature: North American Landscape From Disney to the Exxon Valdez.* Cambridge 1992. Seite 233 ff

NEGEL TIERE, SENSATIONEN BRUNNER FORM-/ZIRCA 1123/9555

architektur Franz Hesse erinnert sic in seinen Beobachtungen berlinischen Lebens an die merkwürdigen Behausunge der Tiere: Liebt das Zebra sein afrikanisches Gehöft, der Büffel sein Borkenpalais?⁷ Die Steine von Bärenzwinger, Vogelhaus und Löwenheim deutet Hessel al Baukastensteine, der Zoo wird in seiner Interpretation zur natürlichen Fortsetzun einer Kinderstube und einem Ort, wo di vorzeitlichen Tierkulte Gelegenheit haben wiederaufzuleben. F. Lichterfeld bezieh sich in einem Artikel der ILLUSTRIRTEN ZEITUNG von 1873 auf die anfänglich vorhanden Verwunderung der Stadtbewohner ob de neuen, ungewohnten Bauwerke: «Was solle diese Thürme mit der flammenden Sonn und den phantastischen Drachen- und Elefantenbildern in einer christlichen Stad wie Berlin?» Diese Frage wurde früher häufig aufgeworfen, zumal von Landleuter welche ihr Weg nach der Stadt an der fremden Heidentempel vorüber führte. Jetzt weiß jedermann in und um Berlin, daß der fremde Heidentempel das neue Elefantenhaus ist. [...] Nicht diesen, sondern dem Publikum zulieb wurde der Neubau so reich ausgestattet, denn selbst dem Elefanten ist eine Portion Moorrüben oder ein Bund Heu lieber als der ganze architektonische und musivische Schmuck seines neuen Hauses, und nun gar erst dem Rhinoceros! ‖ Die stilistische Gestaltung der Bauten steht offensichtlich auch in Zusammenhang mit der Einbindung der zoologischen Gärten in kolonialistische Zusammenhänge. Die Repräsentation fremdkultureller Elemente erlaubt Rückschlüsse auf die Konturen eines rudimentär entwickelten Kosmopolitismus. Das Einbringen von Elementen aus anderen Kulturzusammenhängen markiert den Wandel vom systematischen zum geographisch orientierten Zoo. Wichtigen Einfluß auf die Idee, Tiere in einem baulich-stilistischen Rahmen zu zeigen, der gewisse Zusammenhänge zur Ethnographie der Heimatlandschaften aufweist, hatte der Zoologe Philipp Leopold Martin, in seinem 1878 in Leipzig erschienenen Kompendium DIE PRAXIS DER NATURGESCHICHTE — er maße sich an, es als vollständiges Lehrbuch über das Sammeln lebender und todter Naturkörper zu bezeichnen — rationalisiert Martin dieses Vorgehen als ethnographisch-architektonische Belehrung: Was ist aber nun wohl natürlicher und zugleich lehrreicher, als die Natur in unseren Gärten nach Welttheilen, Zonen und lokalen Verhältnissen aufzustellen? [...] Der Wisent verlangt Wald und der Buffalo die Prairie; und wenn wir dieses thun und in die Prairie noch einen Wigwam als Stall hinsetzen, so belehren wir damit zugleich das Publikum, denn es erhält Bilder, die es niemals vergißt.⁸ Die fremdkulturelle Architektur der Stilbauten — auch wichtiger Bestandteil der großen Weltausstellungen in dieser Phase — wird jeglicher zeitlicher Entwicklung enthoben. Zoodirektor Ludwig Heck schreibt rückblickend im Jahre 1929: Man denke nur, wenn wir

[7] Franz Hessel Spazieren in Berlin Berlin 1929 · Seite 149
[8] Heinz-Georg und Ursula Klös Der Berliner Zoo im Spiegel seiner Bauten 1841–1989. Eine baugeschichtliche und denkmalpflegerische Dokumentation über den Zoologischen Garten Berlin 1990 · Seite 10 · Die anderen Ausführungen über die Architektur stützen sich partiell auf diesen Band

FORM + ZWECK 27
Journal
Designers: Cyan, Berlin
In the pages of this experimental journal, compact columns of justified text are pushed to the outer margins. By marking paragraphs with symbols rather than indents and line breaks, the designers have maximized the density of the text field. Running heads, page numbers, and images are narrow channels cut into a solid wall of text. Footnotes are also treated as justified blocks, turned 90 degrees against the grain of the page.

a

b

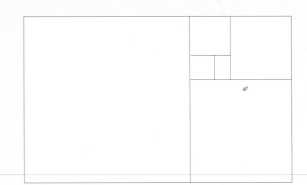

The golden section, which appears in nature as well as in art and design, has many surprising properties. For example, when you remove a square from a golden rectangle, the remainder is another golden rectangle, a process that can be infinitely repeated to create a spiral.

No book about typography would be complete without a discussion of the *golden section*, a ratio (relationship between two numbers) that has been used in Western art and architecture for more than two thousand years. The formula for the golden section is

a : b = b : (a+b).

This means that the smaller of two elements (such as the side of a rectangle) relates to the larger element in the same way that that the larger element relates to the two parts combined. In other words, side *a* is to side *b* as side *b* is to the sum of both sides. Expressed numerically, the golden section is

1 : 1.618

Some graphic designers are fascinated with the golden section and use it to create various grids and page formats—indeed, entire books have been written on the subject. Other designers believe that the golden section is no more valid as a basis for deriving sizes and proportions than other methods, such as beginning from standard industrial paper sizes, or dividing surfaces into halves or squares, or simply picking whole-number page formats and making logical divisions within them.

A grid can be simple or complex, specific or generic, tightly defined or loosely interpreted. Typographic grids are all about control. They establish a system for arranging content within the space of page, screen, or built environment. Designed in response to the internal pressures of content (text, image, data) and the outer edge or frame (page, screen, window), an effective grid is not a rigid formula but a flexible and resilient structure, a skeleton that moves in concert with the muscular mass of content. Grids belong to the technological framework of typography, from the concrete modularity of letterpress to the ubiquitous rulers, guides, and coordinate systems of graphics applications. Although software generates illusions of smooth curves and continuous tones, every digital image or mark is constructed—ultimately—from a grid of neatly bounded blocks. The ubiquitous language of the GUI (graphical user interface) creates a gridded space in which windows overlay windows. In addition to their place in the background of design production, grids have become explicit theoretical tools. Avant-garde designers in the 1910s and 1920s exposed the mechanical grid of letterpress, bringing it to the polemical surface of the page. In Switzerland after World War II, graphic designers built a total design methodology around the typographic grid, hoping to build from it a new and rational social order. The grid has evolved across centuries of typographic evolution. For graphic designers, grids are carefully honed intellectual devices, infused with ideology and ambition, and they are the inescapable mesh that filters, at some level of resolution, nearly every system of writing and reproduction. A grid can be simple or complex, specific or generic, tightly defined or loosely interpreted. Typographic grids are all about control. They establish a system for arranging content within the space of page, screen, or built environment. Designed in response to the internal pressures of content (text, image, data) and the outer edge or frame (page, screen, window), an effective grid is not a rigid formula but a flexible and resilient structure, a skeleton that moves in concert with the muscular mass of content. Grids belong to the technological framework of typography, from the concrete modularity of letterpress to the ubiquitous rulers, guides, and coordinate systems of graphics applications. Although software generates illusions of smooth curves and continuous tones, every digital image or mark is constructed—ultimately—from a grid of neatly bounded blocks. The ubiquitous language of the GUI (graphical user interface) creates a gridded space in which windows overlay

Golden rectangle of text on 8.5 x 11-inch page (U.S. standard)

A grid can be simple or complex, specific or generic, tightly defined or loosely interpreted. Typographic grids are all about control. They establish a system for arranging content within the space of page, screen, or built environment. Designed in response to the internal pressures of content (text, image, data) and the outer edge or frame (page, screen, window), an effective grid is not a rigid formula but a flexible and resilient structure, a skeleton that moves in concert with the muscular mass of content. Grids belong to the technological framework of typography, from the concrete modularity of letterpress to the ubiquitous rulers, guides, and coordinate systems of graphics applications. Although software generates illusions of smooth curves and continuous tones, every digital image or mark is constructed—ultimately—from a grid of neatly bounded blocks. The ubiquitous language of the GUI (graphical user interface) creates a gridded space in which windows overlay windows. In addition to their place in the background of design production, grids have become explicit theoretical tools. Avant-garde designers in the 1910s and 1920s exposed the mechanical grid of letterpress, bringing it to the polemical surface of the page. In Switzerland after World War II, graphic designers built a total design methodology around the typographic grid, hoping to build from it a new and rational social order. The grid has evolved across centuries of typographic evolution. For graphic designers, grids are carefully honed intellectual devices, infused with ideology and ambition, and they are the inescapable mesh that filters, at some level of resolution, nearly every system of writing and reproduction. A grid can be simple or complex, specific or generic, tightly defined or loosely interpreted. Typographic grids are all about control. They establish a system for arranging content within the space of page, screen, or built environment. Designed in response to the internal pressures of content (text, image, data) and the outer edge or frame (page, screen, window), an effective grid is not a rigid formula but a flexible and resilient structure, a skeleton that moves in consert with the muscular mass of content. Grids belong to the technological framework of typography, from the concrete modularity of letterpress to the ubiquitous rulers, guides, and coordinate systems of graphics applications. Although software generates illusions of smooth curves and continuous tones, every digital image or mark is constructed—ultimately—from a grid of neatly bounded blocks. The ubiquitous language of the GUI (graphical user interface) creates a gridded space in which windows overlay windows. In addition to their

Golden rectangle of text on A4 page (European standard, 210 x 297 mm)

Commercial printers generally prefer to work with pages trimmed to even measures rather than with obscure fractions. However, you can float golden rectangles within a page of any trim size.

For a more detailed account of design and the golden section, see Kimberly Elam, *Geometry of Design* (New York: Princeton Architectural Press, 2001). For an emphasis on applying the golden section to typography, see John Kane, *A Type Primer* (London: Laurence King, 2002).

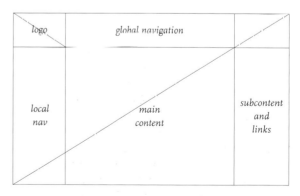

It may well be absurd to base a Web site on the golden section, but here, nonetheless, is a design for one. This wire frame diagram describes a Web page that is 500 x 809 pixels. The "golden screen" is then divided with squares and golden rectangles.

A grid can be simple or complex, specific or generic, tightly defined or loosely interpreted. Typographic grids are all about control. They establish a system for arranging content within the space of page, screen, or built environment. Designed in response to the internal pressures of content (text, image, data) and the outer edge or frame (page, screen, window), an effective grid is not a rigid formula but a flexible and resilient structure, a skeleton that moves in concert with the muscular mass of content. Grids belong to the technological framework of typography, from the concrete modularity of letterpress to the ubiquitous rulers, guides, and coordinate systems of graphics applications. Although software generates illusions of smooth curves and continuous tones, every digital image or mark is constructed—ultimately—from a grid of neatly bounded blocks. The ubiquitous language of the GUI (graphical user interface) creates a gridded space in which windows overlay windows. In addition to their place in the background of design production, grids have become explicit theoretical tools. Avant-garde designers in the 1910s and 1920s exposed the mechanical grid of letterpress, bringing it to the polemical surface of the page. In Switzerland after World War II, graphic designers built a total design methodology around the typographic grid, hoping to build from it a new and rational social order. The grid has evolved across centuries of typographic evolution. For graphic designers, grids are carefully honed intellectual devices, infused with ideology and ambition, and they are the inescapable mesh that filters, at some level of resolution, nearly every system of writing and reproduction. A grid can be simple or complex, specific or generic, tightly defined or loosely interpreted. Typographic grids are all about control. They establish a system for arranging content within the space of page, screen, or built environment. Designed in response to the internal pressures of content (text, image, data) and the outer edge or frame (page, screen, window), an effective grid is not a rigid formula but a flexible and resilient structure, a skeleton that moves in concert with the muscular mass of content. Grids belong to the technological framework of typography, from the concrete modularity of letterpress to the ubiquitous rulers, guides, and coordinate systems of graphics applications. Although software generates illusions of smooth curves and continuous tones, every digital image or mark is constructed—ultimately—from a grid of neatly bounded blocks. The ubiquitous language of the GUI (graphical user interface) creates a gridded space in which windows overlay windows. In addition to their place in the background of design production, grids have become explicit theoretical tools. Avant-garde designers in the 1910s and 1920s exposed the mechanical grid of letterpress, bringing it to the polemical surface of the page. In Switzerland after World War II, graphic designers built a total design methodology around the typographic grid, hoping to build from it a new and rational social order. The grid has evolved across centuries of typographic evolution. For graphic designers, grids are carefully honed intellectual devices, infused with ideology and ambition, and they are the inescapable mesh that filters, at some level of resolution, nearly every system of writing and reproduction. A grid can be simple or complex, specific or generic, tightly defined or loosely interpreted. Typographic grids are all about control. They establish a system for arranging content within the space of page, screen, or built environment. Designed in response to the internal pressures of content (text, image, data) and the outer edge or frame (page, screen, window), an effective grid is not a rigid formula but a flexible and resilient structure, a skeleton that moves in concert with the muscular mass of content. Grids belong to the technological framework of typography, from the

This standard, 8.5 x 11-inch page has even margins all the way around. It is a highly economical, but not very interesting, design.

GRID SYSTEMS   PAGE ONE

A grid can be simple or complex, specific or generic, tightly defined or loosely interpreted. Typographic grids are all about control. They establish a system for arranging content within the space of page, screen, or built environment. Designed in response to the internal pressures of content (text, image, data) and the outer edge or frame (page, screen, window), an effective grid is not a rigid formula but a flexible and resilient structure, a skeleton that moves in concert with the muscular mass of content. Grids belong to the technological framework of typography, from the concrete modularity of letterpress to the ubiquitous rulers, guides, and coordinate systems of graphics applications. Although software generates illusions of smooth curves and continuous tones, every digital image or mark is constructed—ultimately—from a grid of neatly bounded blocks. The ubiquitous language of the GUI (graphical user interface) creates a gridded space in which windows overlay windows. In addition to their place in the background of design production, grids have become explicit theoretical tools. Avant-garde designers in the 1910s and 1920s exposed the mechanical grid of letterpress, bringing it to the polemical surface of the page. In Switzerland after World War II, graphic designers built a total design methodology around the typographic grid, hoping to build from it a new and rational social order. The grid has evolved across centuries of typographic evolution. For graphic designers, grids are carefully honed intellectual devices, infused with ideology and ambition, and they are the inescapable mesh that filters, at some level of resolution, nearly every system of writing and reproduction. A grid can be simple or complex, specific or generic, tightly defined or loosely interpreted. Typographic grids are all about control. They establish a system for arranging content within the space of page, screen, or built environment. Designed in response to the internal pressures of content (text, image, data) and the outer edge or frame (page, screen, window), an effective grid is not a rigid formula but a flexible and resilient structure, a skeleton that moves in concert with the muscular mass of content. Grids belong to the technological framework of typography, from the concrete modularity of letterpress to the ubiquitous rulers, guides, and coordinate systems of graphics applications. Although software generates illusions of smooth curves and continuous tones, every digital image or mark is constructed—ultimately—from a grid of neatly bounded blocks. The ubiquitous language of the GUI (graphical user interface) creates a gridded space in which windows overlay windows. In addition to their place in the background of design production, grids have become explicit theoretical tools. Avant-garde designers in the 1910s and 1920s exposed the mechanical grid of letterpress, bringing it to

This page is an inch shorter than a standard US office sheet. The text block is a square, leaving margins of varying size.

Every time you open a new document in Quark XPress or Adobe InDesign, you are prompted to create a grid. (Microsoft Word, on the other hand, doesn't ask; it just makes a grid for you.) The simplest grid consists of a single column of text surounded by margins.

By asking for page dimensions and margin widths from the outset, layout programs encourage you to design your page from the *outside in.* (The text column is the space left over when the margins have been subtracted.)

Alternatively, you can design your page from the inside out, by setting your margins to zero and then positioning guidelines and text boxes on a blank page. This allows you to experiment with the margins and columns rather than making a commitment as soon as you open a new document. You can add guidelines to a master page after they meet your satisfaction.

GRID SYSTEMS   PAGE ONE   GRID SYSTEMS   PAGE ONE

A grid can be simple or complex, specific or generic, tightly defined or loosely interpreted. Typographic grids are all about control. They establish a system for arranging content within the space of page, screen, or built environment. Designed in response to the internal pressures of content (text, image, data) and the outer edge or frame (page, screen, window), an effective grid is not a rigid formula but a flexible and resilient structure, a skeleton that moves in concert with the muscular mass of content. Grids belong to the technological framework of typography, from the concrete modularity of letterpress to the ubiquitous rulers, guides, and coordinate systems of graphics applications. Although software generates illusions of smooth curves and continuous tones, every digital image or mark is constructed—ultimately—from a grid of neatly bounded blocks. The ubiquitous language of the GUI (graphical user interface) creates a gridded space in which windows overlay windows. In addition to their place in the background of design production, grids have become explicit theoretical tools. Avant-garde designers in the 1910s and 1920s exposed the mechanical grid of letterpress, bringing it to the polemical surface of the page. In Switzerland after World War II, graphic designers built a total design methodology around the typographic grid, hoping to build from it a new and rational social order. The grid has evolved across centuries of typographic evolution. For graphic designers, grids are carefully honed intellectual devices, infused with ideology and ambition, and they are the inescapable mesh that filters, at some level of resolution, nearly every system of writing and reproduction. A grid can be simple or complex, specific or generic, tightly defined or loosely interpreted. Typographic grids are all about control. They establish a system for arranging content within the space of page, screen, or built environment. Designed in response to the internal pressures of content (text, image, data) and the outer edge or frame (page, screen, window), an effective grid is not a rigid formula but a flexible and resilient structure, a skeleton that moves in concert with the muscular mass of content. Grids belong to the technological framework of typography, from the concrete modularity of letterpress to the ubiquitous rulers, guides, and coordinate systems of graphics applications. Although software generates illusions of smooth curves and continuous tones, every digital image or mark is constructed—ultimately—from a grid of neatly bounded blocks. The ubiquitous language of the GUI (graphical user interface) creates a gridded space in which windows overlay windows. In addition to their place in the background of design production, grids have become explicit theoretical tools. Avant-garde designers in the 1910s and 1920s exposed the mechanical grid of letterpress, bringing it to

A grid can be simple or complex, specific or generic, tightly defined or loosely interpreted. Typographic grids are all about control. They establish a system for arranging content within the space of page, screen, or built environment. Designed in response to the internal pressures of content (text, image, data) and the outer edge or frame (page, screen, window), an effective grid is not a rigid formula but a flexible and resilient structure, a skeleton that moves in concert with the muscular mass of content. Grids belong to the technological framework of typography, from the concrete modularity of letterpress to the ubiquitous rulers, guides, and coordinate systems of graphics applications. Although software generates illusions of smooth curves and continuous tones, every digital image or mark is constructed—ultimately—from a grid of neatly bounded blocks. The ubiquitous language of the GUI (graphical user interface) creates a gridded space in which windows overlay windows. In addition to their place in the background of design production, grids have become explicit theoretical tools. Avant-garde designers in the 1910s and 1920s exposed the mechanical grid of letterpress, bringing it to the polemical surface of the page. In Switzerland after World War II, graphic designers built a total design methodology around the typographic grid, hoping to build from it a new and rational social order. The grid has evolved across centuries of typographic evolution. For graphic designers, grids are carefully honed intellectual devices, infused with ideology and ambition, and they are the inescapable mesh that filters, at some level of resolution, nearly every system of writing and reproduction. A grid can be simple or complex, specific or generic, tightly defined or loosely interpreted. Typographic grids are all about control. They establish a system for arranging content within the space of page, screen, or built environment. Designed in response to the internal pressures of content (text, image, data) and the outer edge or frame (page, screen, window), an effective grid is not a rigid formula but a flexible and resilient structure, a skeleton that moves in concert with the muscular mass of content. Grids belong to the technological framework of typography, from the concrete modularity of letterpress to the ubiquitous rulers, guides, and coordinate systems of graphics applications. Although software generates illusions of smooth curves and continuous tones, every digital image or mark is constructed—ultimately—from a grid of neatly bounded blocks. The ubiquitous language of the GUI (graphical user interface) creates a gridded space in which windows overlay windows. In addition to their place in the background of design production, grids have become explicit theoretical tools. Avant-garde designers in the 1910s and 1920s exposed the mechanical grid of letterpress, bringing it to

In this symmetrical double-page spread, the inside margins are wider than the outside margins, creating more open space at the spine of the book.

Books and magazines should be designed as *spreads* (facing pages). The two-page spread, rather than the individual page, is the main unit of design. Left and right margins become inside and outside margins. Page layout programs assume that the inside margins are the same on both the left- and right-hand pages, yielding a symmetrical, mirror-image spread. You are free, however, to set your own margins and create an asymmetrical spread.

In this asymmetrical layout, the left margin is always wider than the right margin, whether it appears along the inside or outside edge of the page.

Grid systems

A grid can be simple or complex, specific or generic, tightly defined or loosely interpreted. Typographic grids are all about control. They establish a system for arranging content within the space of page, screen, or built environment. Designed in response to the internal pressures of content (text, image, data) and the outer edge or frame (page, screen, window), an effective grid is not a rigid formula but a flexible and resilient structure, a skeleton that moves in concert with the muscular mass of content. Grids belong to the technological framework of typography, from the concrete modularity of letterpress to the ubiquitous rulers, guides, and coordinate systems of graphics applications. Although software generates illusions of smooth curves and continuous tones, every digital image or mark is constructed—ultimately—from a grid of neatly bounded blocks. The ubiquitous language of the GUI (graphical user interface) creates a gridded space in which windows overlay windows. In addition to their place in the background of design production, grids have become explicit theoretical tools. Avant-garde designers in the 1910s and 1920s exposed the mechanical grid of letterpress, bringing it to the polemical surface of the page. In

The typographic grid is a proportional regulator for composition, tables, pictures, etc. It is a formal programme to accommodate x unknown items. The typographic grid is a proportional regulator for composition, tables, pictures, etc. It is a formal programme to accommodate x unknown items.

There are numerous ways to use a basic column grid. Here, one column has been reserved for images and captions, and the others for text.

In this variation, images and text share column space.

While single-column grids work well for simple documents, multi-column grids provide flexible formats for publications that have a complex hierarchy or that integrate text and illustrations. The more columns you create, the more flexible your grid becomes. You can use the grid to articulate the hierarchy of the publication by creating zones for different kinds of content. A text or image can occupy a single column or it can span several. Not all the space has to be filled.

Elements of varying width are staggered within the structure of the grid.

A horizontal band divides a text zone from an image zone. Elements gravitate towards this line, which provides an internal structure for the page.

In addition to creating vertical zones with the columns of the grid, you can also divide the page horizontally. For example, an area across the top can be reserved for images and captions, and body text can "hang" from a common line. In architecture, a horizontal reference point like this is called a *datum*.

Columns of text hang from a datum, falling downward with an uneven rag across the bottom.

Ifang Leisalpa
(Schloss),
2090 Meter

und verdichtet, wie dies im Betonbau üblich ist. Da der Beton
bei diesem Vorgang die Vor- und Rücksprünge der Rückseite
der Steinplattenwand umfliesst, entstand eine vorzügliche
Verzahnung und Verbindung der beiden Materialien Kunststein
(Beton) und Naturstein.

Allerdings konnten die Wände nicht in ihrer ganzen Höhe
auf einmal hintergossen werden. Das musste in Höhenetappen
von 50 cm erfolgen. Erst wenn der Beton einer Lage eine bestimm-
te Festigkeit erreicht und sich mit dem Mauerwerk verbunden
hatte, konnte die nächste Lage von 50 cm darüber betoniert
werden. Eine höhere Schüttmasse von flüssigem Beton hätte
die freistehenden Steinplattenwände seitlich weggedrückt.

Insgesamt wurden für die Wände der Therme 450 m³ oder
1300 Tonnen Valser Quarzitplatten zu 3100 m² Wandfläche in
20 Schichten pro m² verarbeitet. Die Länge aller verwendeten
Plattenstreifen zusammen ergibt ein Total von 62.000 Lauf-
metern, was der Strecke von Vals nach Haldenstein entspricht.
Peter Zumthor

Valser Quarzit	Boden	Fugen und Mörtelmasse	Grotten
Druckfestigkeit: etwa 217 N/mm²	Breiten der Bahnen: 8–110 cm	EMACO R 304 BARRA 80 Firma	Trinkstein: polierte Quader
Rohdichte: 2.698 kg/m³	Längen: bis 3,20 m, je Platte zum Teil	MBT	Eckverbin- dungen, Schwel-	aufeinander- geschichte Grösse
Wasseraufnahme- koeffizient:	über 3 m² in einer Stärke von 2 cm	len, Sturzplatten, Treppenunter-	etwa 0,5–1 m³ Quellgrotte:
Masse –% 0,25	Oberflächen:	sichte und Tritte,	gebrochener
Gefräste Stein- platten: Stärken	poliert, gefräst, gestockt, ge-	Sitze als einzel- ne Werkstücke	Stein im Innern Schwitzstein:
6, 3, 4, 7 und 3,1cm	schliffen in allen	gefertigt	minimale	eingefärbter und
Toleranz: 1 mm	Möglichkeiten	Toleranzen (weit	polierter Beton
Breiten: 12–30 cm	und einer Fugen-	unter SIA-Norm)	Steininsel:
Längen: bis 3,20 m	breite von 1 mm	beim Schneiden	grossformatige
über 60.000 lfm		und Vermauern	gespaltene Platten
Fugenbreite:		der Steine, wie zum	bis zu 3 m² je
etwa 2 mm		Beispiel auf 6 m	Platte
		Höhe weniger als	
		5 mm Toleranz	

STEIN UND VASSER,
WINTER 2003|04
Booklet, 2003
Designer: Clemens Schedler,
Büro für konkrete Gestaltung
Publisher: Hotel Therme,
Switzerland
*This publication for a spa in
Switzerland uses a five-column
grid. The main text fills a four-
column block, and the smaller
texts occupy single columns.*

General
Non-Fiction

Art

Photography

Collector's
Editions

Film

Architecture

220 × 156 mm
8⅝ × 6⅛ inches
240 pp
c.80 b&w illus.

Paperback
0 7148 3164 6

£ 14.95   UK
$ 24.95   US
€ 24.95   EUR
$ 39.95   CAN
$ 49.95   AUS

Béla Bartók

Kenneth Chalmers

- Sets Béla Bartók (1881–1945) and his work in the context of his homeland Hungary and his native city Budapest, where he lived for most of his adult life
- Covers the full range of his work from his early explorations of the folklore of Hungary to his Third Piano Concerto composed on his deathbed in the United States
- Brings out the singular nature of his genius and the originality of his contribution to music

Kenneth Chalmers is an author, translator and composer who has written on Bartók, Berg, Stravinsky, Verdi and Weill, and collaborated on Decca's 20-volume Mozart Almanac

Design

Fashion & Contemporary Culture

Decorative Arts

Music & Performing Arts
20th Century Composers

Video

Index

220 × 156 mm
8¹⁄₂ × 6¹⁄₄ inches
240 pp
c.80 b&w illus.

Paperback
0 7148 3203 0

£ 14.95 UK
$ 24.95 US
€ 24.95 EUR
$ 39.95 CAN
$ 49.95 AUS

The Beatles

Allan Kozinn

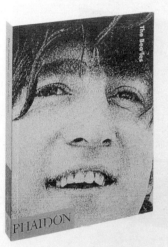

- Follows the extraordinary development of the four self-taught musicians from Liverpool from their beginnings until the break-up in 1970
- Examines why the innovative music of the Beatles – created, at least initially, as ephemera – has remained so durable
- Considers not only the commercially released disks but also studio outtakes, demos, unreleased recordings and broadcast performances
- Sets the group's evolution against the backdrop of the popular culture explosion of the 1960s

Allan Kozinn has written musical criticism for the *New York Times* since 1977 and won ASCAP awards for his work, including the book *Mischa Elman and the Romantic Style*

'A well-rounded, readable account. Makes a convincing case for putting the Beatles on the shelf between Bartók and Boulez.' *(The Sunday Times)*

PHAIDON. FALL 2003
Catalogue, 2003
Designer: Hans Dieter Reichert
Publisher: Phaidon
Photograph: Dan Meyers
This catalogue for a book publisher provides a rational and elegant structure for displaying hundreds of different books, each one presented as a physical object annotated with documentary data. The margins act as a navigational interface for the catalogue. Divisions occur both horizontally and vertically.

> Play serves learning though experimentation without risk. Learning occurs through quick, imprecise actions, conducted within understood rules of a game, and free from threat or consummation. Play does not use up so much as build.

military-industrial world of computing, one important way to do so is to play.

Play takes many forms. For example, it can be individual or social. According to one classic taxonomy, individual play includes pursuit of sensations, exercise of motor apparatus and experimentation with higher mental powers. This mental play includes exercise of attention, emotion and will. Attention play includes tests of memory, imagination, focus and reason. On the other hand, social play includes fighting and rivalry, loving and courtship, imitation and status seeking. Imitative play includes movements, drama, behavioural constructions and emulation of inner states. [2]

Crafts and craft learning embrace quite a range of these playful forms. Arguably, no productive process combines so many so well. Sensation, skilled motion, attention, involvement, will — all must be balanced, and this is the basis for craft as recreation. Craft learning is a form of imitative social learning. Movements are physical skills taught directly, whether by demonstration or coaching. Drama is a lesser component here, although it may be understood in the willful suspension of disbelief that allows participation in an abstract medium. Constructions are the artifacts. They are the plastic play, the visual examples, the operational learning. Finally the inner state is the patience, reflectivity and intent that distinguish the master.

Play serves learning though experimentation without risk. Play often lacks any immediately obvious aim other than the pursuit of stimulation, but functions almost instinctively to serve the process of development. Learning occurs through quick, imprecise actions, conducted within understood rules of a game, and free from threat or consummation. Play does not use up so much as build. One thing it

builds is common sense. Play's endlessly variable series of awkward, exaggerated motions seeks out the approximate arena for later development of true competence.

There is much to be said for play in a medium. If a medium is defined by its affordances and constraints, then learning consists of exploring these properties. Experimentation is especially useful for becoming familiar with constraints: we learn from our mistakes. We must accept that beginning work in a new medium will be full of setbacks. There will also be fortuitous discoveries, however particularly of affordances. Design is not only invention, but also sensitivity to a medium. Craft cannot be merely in service of technique, or of inappropriately conceived ends. The craftsman must begin to feel something about the artifacts, and only certain moves will feel right.

Of course when it comes to computation, we all must learn. In a sense, we're all children— the medium is *that* new. And of course, the most fluent experts here are often quite young. As all of us learn about this promising new domain, a chain of developments should be clear: play shapes learning; learning shapes the mind; mental structures shape software; and software data structures afford work and play.

Structure and Improvisation

The master at play improvises. Consider the jazz pianist. In *Ways of the Hand — The Organization of Improvised Conduct* (1978), the musician David Sudnow gives us a rare description of otherwise tacit knowledge in action. Improvising on a piece takes much more talent than simply playing from a notation or learning by rote, Sudnow explains. Moreover, improvising begins with a sense of structure, from which it builds a cognitive map. For example, the 'way in' to an arpeggio is mentally mapped. The structure of the keyboard presents a physical map of a chord, which may be modified in countless ways by physical moves. One could play the adjacent keys, for example, or one could translate by any arbitrary interval. One could transpose or invert. One could change the order in which the notes were played, or the

2 Karl Groos, *The Play of Man.* New York: Appleton and Co., 1901

If/Then   Discovery in Digital Craft   Malcolm McCullough   135
             keyboards, digital and musical   4/8

the same pitches as the first, the doubled back and went fast in again, but over different pitches... There were innumerable variations possible; looking at 'structure' in this way and corresponding to various continuity practices, ways of the hand were cultivated that were suited to the performance of such manoeuvres... Transposition of such a figure to a new segment and correct repetition with respect to pitch, without slowing it down or slowing down parts of it, involved coping with the topography of the terrain by the hand as a negotiative organ with various potentials and limitations. [3]

tempo, or the attack and decay. Of course one could substitute dominant, major and minor chords.

Sudnow argues that because these variations are sequences of physical positions, they are learned as active skills no longer necessary to be understood at a mental level. Each becomes a handful. That the hand gets a hold of a variation on a chord is indicated by observed tendencies to start into particular sequences with certain fingers on certain keys. The manoeuvre is known by the hand, and the mind only maps the way in. The ability to modify the run note by note — which would require conscious attention — only comes later. Even without attentive intellectual guidance, however, the natural tendency of the hand is not to repeat itself, even in a series of figural repetitions. Thus once a sufficient repertoire of runs is learned, this tendency inherently ensures a richness to the sound. The hand searches its territory for sequences, which process replaces a faithfulness to the score, and that makes jazz. For example:

> The new run could be in various other ways only 'essentially related' to the preceding run. Say the first started slow and went up fast, then doubled back and went fast again, while the second started slowly and came back down through

Although jazz is the obvious case, it is hardly alone. Improvisation plays a role in many contemporary practices, and in many traditional crafts. Few of these worlds employ such a singular instrument as the piano; few are able to turn so much over to the hands, but all involve playful response to a structure. For example, of industrial design, Herbert Read insisted that "Art implies values more various than those determined by practical necessity." [4] As a modernist and industrialist, he felt admiration for fundamental structural laws, such as the golden section also admired by his contemporary Le Corbusier. He was convinced, however, that metrical irregularities based on a governing structure, rather than slavish adherence to the laws in their precision, was the basis for pleasurable expression. He cited Ruskin's line that "All beautiful lines are drawn under mathematical laws organically transgressed." [5] He held that this was the case even in the useful (industrial) arts.

Consider the case of processing a digital photograph. The makeup of the raster image file, the various tone scale and filtration operators, provides a very clear structure in which to work but demands no particular order of operation. The complex microstructure of the sampled pixels provides a sub-

> The natural tendency of the hand is not to repeat itself, even in a series of figural repetitions. Thus once a sufficient repertoire of runs is learned, this tendency inherently ensures a richness to the sound. The hand searches its territory for sequences, which process replaces a faithfulness to the score, and that makes jazz.

3 David Sudnow, Ways of the Hand—The Organization of Improvised Conduct, Cambridge, MA: Harvard University Press, 1978, p 7
4 Herbert Read, Art and Industry—The Principles of Industrial Design New York: Horizon Press, 1954 [1934]
5 Ibid.

IF/THEN PLAY: DESIGN IMPLICATIONS OF NEW MEDIA
Book, 1999
Designers: Mevis and Van Deursen
Editor: Jan Abrams
Publisher: Netherlands Design Institute
Photograph: Dan Meyers
In this book about new media, a two-column grid contains the main body of text. The pull quotes, running across two columns, are framed in thinly ruled boxes that suggest the overlapping "windows" on a computer screen. The top margin, which resembles the tool bar in a browser, provides an interface to the book.

DESIGNING PROGRAMS
Grid diagram, 1963 (redrawn)
Designer: Karl Gerstner
Arthur Niggli, Zurich

This square grid consists of six vertical columns and six horizontal modules, overlayed by grids of one, two, three, and four units.

Vertically, the grid is governed by a 10-point measure, which would determine the spacing of type from baseline to baseline.

Grid systems

A grid can be simple or complex, specific or generic, tightly defined or loosely interpreted. Typographic grids are all about control. They establish a system for arranging content within the space of page, screen, or built environment. Designed in response to the internal pressures of content (text, image, data) and the outer edge or frame (page, screen, window), an effective grid is not a rigid formula but a flexible and resilient structure, a skeleton that moves in concert with the muscular mass of content. Grids belong to the technological framework of typography, from the concrete modularity of letterpress to the ubiquitous rulers, guides, and coordinate systems of graphics applications. Although software generates illusions of smooth curves and continuous tones, every digital image or mark is constructed—ultimately—from a grid of neatly bounded blocks. The ubiquitous language of the GUI (graphical user interface) creates a gridded space in which windows overlay windows. In addition to their place in the background of design production, grids have become explicit theoretical tools. Avant-garde designers in the 1910s and 1920s exposed the grid of letterpress, bringing it to the polemical surface of the page. In Switzerland after World War II, graphic designers built a total design methodology around the typographic grid, hoping to build from it a new and rational social order. The grid has evolved across centuries of typographic evolution. For graphic designers, grids are carefully honed intellectual devices, infused with ideology and ambition, and they are the inescapable mesh that filters, at some level of resolution, nearly every system of writing and

The typographic grid is a proportional regulator for composition, tables, pictures, etc. It is a formal programme to accommodate x unknown items. The typographic grid is a proportional regulator for composition, tables, pictures, etc. It is a formal programme to accommodate x unknown items.

The typographic grid is a proportional regulator for composition, tables, pictures, etc. It is a formal programme to accommodate x unknown items. The typographic grid is a proportional regulator for composition, tables, pictures, etc. It is a formal programme to accommodate x unknown items.

The typographic grid is a proportional regulator for composition, tables, pictures, etc. It is a formal programme to accommodate x unknown items. The typographic grid is a proportional regulator for composition, tables, pictures, etc. It is a formal programme to accommodate x unknown items.

This modular grid has four columns and four rows. An image or a text block can occupy one or more modules.

Grid systems

A grid can be simple or complex, specific or generic, tightly defined or loosely interpreted. Typographic grids are all about control. They establish a system for arranging content within the space of page, screen, or built environment. Designed in response to the internal pressures of content (text, image, data) and the outer edge or frame (page, screen, window), an effective grid is not a rigid formula but a flexible and resilient structure, a skeleton that moves in concert with the muscular mass of content. Grids belong to the technological framework of typography, from the concrete modularity of letterpress to the ubiquitous rulers, guides, and coordinate systems of graphics applications. Although software generates illusions of smooth curves and continuous tones, every digital image or mark is constructed—ultimately— from a grid of neatly bounded blocks. The ubiquitous language of the GUI (graphical user interface) creates a gridded space in which windows overlay windows. In addition to their place in the background of design production.

A grid can be simple or complex, specific or generic, tightly defined or loosely interpreted. Typographic grids are all about control. They establish a system for arranging content within the space of page, screen, or built environment. Designed in response to the internal pressures of content (text, image, data) and the outer edge or frame (page, screen, window), an effective grid is not a rigid formula but a flexible and resilient structure, a skeleton that moves in concert with the muscular mass of content. Grids belong to the technological framework of typography, from the concrete modularity of letterpress to the ubiquitous rulers, guides, and coordinate systems of graphics applications. Although software generates illusions of smooth curves and continuous tones, every digital image or mark is constructed—ultimately—from a grid of neatly bounded blocks. The ubiquitous language of the GUI (graphical user interface) creates a gridded space in which windows overlay windows. In addition to their place in the background of

The typographic grid is a proportional regulator for composition, tables, pictures, etc. It is a formal programme to accommodate x unknown items. The typographic grid is a proportional regulator for composition, tables, pictures, etc. It is a formal programme to accommodate x unknown items.

The typographic grid is a proportional regulator for composition, tables, pictures, etc. It is a formal programme to accommodate x unknown items. The typographic grid is a proportional regulator for composition, tables, pictures, etc. It is a formal programme to accommodate x unknown items.

Endless variations are possible.

A modular grid has consistent horizontal divisions from top to bottom, in addition to vertical divisions from left to right. These modules govern the placement and cropping of pictures as well as text. In the 1950s and 1960s, Swiss graphic designers including Karl Gerstner, Emil Ruder, and Josef Müller-Brockmann devised modular grid systems like the one shown here.

Create the horizontal divisions by laying a "type ruler" along the left edge of the page. Using this ruler, position guidelines corresponding to the line spacing (leading) of the type.

A grid can be simple or complex, specific or generic, tightly defined or loosely interpreted. Typographic grids are all about control. They establish a system for arranging content within the space of page, screen, or built environment. Designed in response to the internal pressures of content (text, image, data) and the outer edge or frame (page, screen,

Grid systems

A grid can be simple or complex, specific or generic, tightly defined or loosely interpreted. Typographic grids are all about control. The system for arranging content within the space of page, screen, environment. Designed in response to the internal pressures of (text, image, data) and the outer edge or frame (page, screen, w effective grid is not a rigid formula but a flexible and resilient s skeleton that moves in concert with the muscular mass of cont belong to the technological framework of typography, from the modularity of letterpress to the ubiquitous rulers, guides, and systems of graphics applications. Although software generates smooth curves and continuous tones, every digital image or m constructed—ultimately—from a grid of neatly bounded blocks ubiquitous language of the GUI (graphical user interface) create space in which windows overlay windows. In addition to their background of design production, grids have become explicit th tools. Avant-garde designers in the 1910s and 1920s exposed th mechanical grid of letterpress, bringing it to the polemical surf

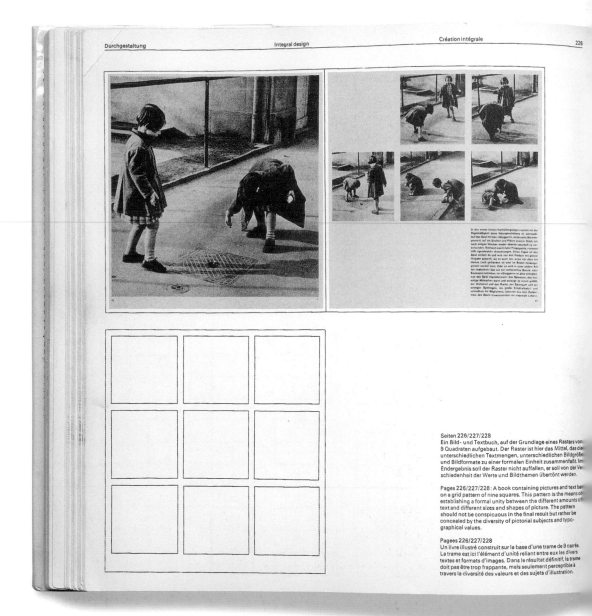

Seiten 226/227/228
Ein Bild- und Textbuch, auf der Grundlage eines Rasters von
9 Quadraten aufgebaut. Der Raster ist hier das Mittel, das die
unterschiedlichen Textmengen, unterschiedlichen Bildgrößen
und Bildformate zu einer formalen Einheit zusammenfaßt. Im
Endergebnis soll der Raster nicht auffallen, er soll von der Ver-
schiedenheit der Werte und Bildthemen übertönt werden.

Pages 226/227/228 : A book containing pictures and text based
on a grid pattern of nine squares. This pattern is the means of
establishing a formal unity between the different amounts of
text and different sizes and shapes of picture. The pattern
should not be conspicuous in the final result but rather be
concealed by the diversity of pictorial subjects and typographical values.

Pagees 226/227/228
Un livre illustré construit sur la base d'une trame de 9 carrés.
La trame est ici l'élément d'unité reliant entre eux les divers
textes et formats d'images. Dans le résultat définitif, la trame
doit pas être trop frappante, mais seulement perceptible à
travers la diversité des valeurs et des sujets d'illustration.

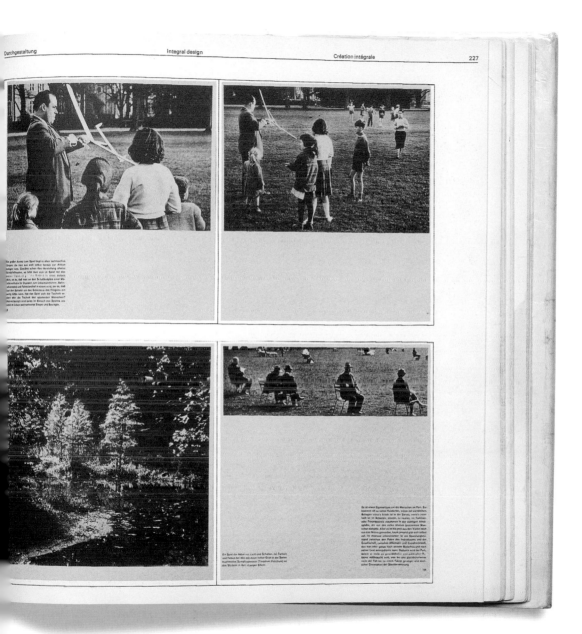

TYPOGRAPHY
Book, 1967
Designer and author:
Emil Ruder
Publisher: Arthur Niggli
Photograph: Dan Meyers

In this classic design text,
Emil Ruder demonstrates the
use of a modular grid.

Common typographic disorders

Various forms of dysfunction appear among populations exposed to typography for long periods of time. Listed here are a number of frequently observed afflictions.

typophilia
An excessive attachment to and fascination with the shape of letters, often to the exclusion of other interests and object choices. Typophiliacs usually die penniless and alone.

typophobia
The irrational dislike of letterforms, often marked by a preference for icons, dingbats, and—in fatal cases—bullets and daggers. The fears of the typophobe can often be quieted (but not cured) by steady doses of Helvetica and Times Roman.

typochondria
A persistent anxiety that one has selected the wrong typeface. This condition is often paired with okd (optical kerning disorder), the need to constantly adjust and readjust the spaces between letters.

Common
typographic
disorders

Various forms of dysfunction appear among populations exposed to typography for long periods of time. Listed here are a number of frequently observed afflictions.

typophilia

An excessive attachment to and fascination with the shape of letters, often to the exclusion of other interests and object choices. Typophiliacs usually die penniless and alone.

typophobia

The irrational dislike of letterforms, often marked by a preference for icons, dingbats, and—in fatal cases—bullets and daggers. The fears of the typophobe can often be quieted (but not cured) by steady doses of Helvetica

typochondria

A persistent anxiety that one has selected the wrong typeface. This condition is often paired with OKD (optical kerning disorder), the need to constantly adjust and readjust the spaces between letters.

Use a modular grid to arrange a text in as many ways as you can. By employing just one size of type, flush left only, you will construct a typographic hierarchy exclusively by means of spatial arrangement. To make the project more complex, begin adding variables such as weight, size, and alignment.

Common
typographic
disorders

Various forms of dysfunction appear among populations exposed to typography for long periods of time. Listed here are a number of frequently observed afflictions.

typophilia
An excessive attachment to and fascination with the shape of letters, often to the exclusion of other interests and object choices. Typophiliacs usually die penniless and alone.

typophobia
The irrational dislike of letterforms, often marked by a preference for icons, dingbats, and—in fatal cases—bullets and daggers. The fears of the typophobe can often be quieted (but not cured) by steady doses of Helvetica and Times Roman.

typochondria
A persistent anxiety that one has selected the wrong typeface. This condition is often paired with OKD (optical kerning disorder), the need to constantly adjust and readjust the spaces between letters.

Top-left quadrant

Common typographic disorders		Various forms of dysfunction appear among populations exposed to typography for long periods of time. Listed here are a number of frequently observed afflictions.
	typophilia	An excessive attachment to and fascination with the shape of letters, often to the exclusion of other interests and object choices. Typophiliacs usually die penniless and alone.
	typophobia	The irrational dislike of letterforms, often marked by a preference for icons, dingbats, and—in fatal cases—bullets and daggers. The fears of the typophobe can often be quieted (but not cured) by steady doses of Helvetica and Times Roman.
	typochondria	A persistent anxiety that one has selected the wrong typeface. This condition is often paired with OKD (optical kerning disorder), the need to constantly adjust and readjust the spaces between letters.

Top-right quadrant

Common typographic disorders			
	typophilia	typophobia	typochondria
Various forms of dysfunction appear among populations exposed to typography for long periods of time. Listed here are a number of frequently observed afflictions.	An excessive attachment to and fascination with the shape of letters, often to the exclusion of other interests and object choices. Typophiliacs usually die penniless and alone.	The irrational dislike of letterforms, often marked by a preference for icons, dingbats, and—in fatal cases—bullets and daggers. The fears of the typophobe can often be quieted (but not cured) by steady doses of Helvetica and Times Roman.	A persistent anxiety that one has selected the wrong typeface. This condition is often paired with OKD (optical kerning disorder), the need to constantly adjust and readjust the spaces between letters.

Bottom-left quadrant

typophilia

An excessive attachment to and fascination with the shape of letters, often to the exclusion of other interests and object choices. Typophiliacs usually die penniless and alone.

Various forms of dysfunction appear among populations exposed to typography for long periods of time. Listed here are a number of frequently observed afflictions.

typophobia

The irrational dislike of letterforms, often marked by a preference for icons, dingbats, and—in fatal cases—bullets and daggers. The fears of the typophobe can often be quieted (but not cured) by steady doses of Helvetica and Times Roman.

A persistent anxiety that one has selected the wrong typeface. This condition is often paired with okd (optical kerning disorder), the need to constantly adjust and readjust the spaces between letters.

typochondria

Common typographic disorders

Bottom-right quadrant

Common typographic disorders

Various forms of dysfunction appear among populations exposed to typography for long periods of time. Listed here are a number of frequently observed afflictions.

typophilia

An excessive attachment to and fascination with the shape of letters, often to the exclusion of other interests and object choices. Typophiliacs usually die penniless and alone.

typophobia

The irrational dislike of letterforms, often marked by a preference for icons, dingbats, and—in fatal cases—bullets and daggers. The fears of the typophobe can often be quieted (but not cured) by steady doses of Helvetica and Times Roman.

typochondria

A persistent anxiety that one has selected the wrong typeface. This condition is often paired with okd (optical kerning disorder), the need to constantly adjust and readjust the spaces between letters.

Shape	Cereal	Year Introduced	Market Share	Price per lb	Maker	Sugar	Fiber	Protein	Sodium
ORTHOGONAL	SHREDDED WHEAT	94	15	3.01	P	1	4	94	0
	RICE CHEX	41	14	4.39	G	2	0	1	280
	FR. SHREDDED WHEAT	55	20	2.94	P	7	3	2	6
	FROSTED MINI-WHEAT	57	15	3.01	K	1	4	4	
	LIFE	62	15	3.01	Q	6	2	3	160
	CRUNCHY CORN BRAN	75	—	3.71	Q	7	6	2	280
	CR…	83							
FLAKE	CORN FLAKE	02	2	1.98	K	2	1	1	330
	WHEATIE	24	21	2.48	G	4	3	3	220
	RAISIN BRAN	28	5	2.44	K	10	4	2	190
	FROSTED FLAKE	52	4	2.93	K	12	1	2	240
	SPECIAL K	55	12	4.92	K	12	1	2	240
	TOTAL	61	37	5.32	G	5	3	3	200
	…O	7.							
GRAIN	PUFFED RICE	02	—	5.98	Q	0	0	2	0
	PUFFED WHEAT	04	—	5.98	Q	0	0	2	0
	RICE KRISPIE	28	3	3.82	K	12	2	200	200
	CORN POP	50	16	2.66	K	12	0	1	120
	SUGAR SMACKS	54	—	2.21	K	16	1	2	60
	COCOA KRISPIES	58	31	2.87	K	12	0	2	200
	F…	6.							
ROUND	KIX	37	22	5.67	G	3	1	2	270
	CHEERIO	41	1	2.66	G	12	3	3	290
	COCOA PUFF	58	24	2.90	G	14	0	1	190
	FROOT LOOP	63	7	3.18	K	13	1	1	140
	APPLE JACK	64	18	2.01	K	14	1	1	130
	HONEY NUT CHEERIO	79	6	3.64	G	11	2	2	280
	H…	8.							
FAKE	TRIX	54	14	4.39	G	13	1	1	200
	ALPHABITS	57	—	3.75	P	14	0	2	160
	FRANKENBERRY	61	15	3.01	G	14	0	0	210
	LUCKY CHARMS	64	11	4.56	G	13	1	1	210
	CRUNCHBERRIES	68	11	4.25	Q	14	1	1	210
	KABOOM	69	—	3.98	G	6	1	3	280
	H…	7.							

YEAR INTRODUCED **00**
MARKET SHARE (15)
PRICE PER LB (3.01)
MAKER (P)

SUGAR (1)
FIBER (4)
PROTEIN (4)
SODIUM (0)

(G) GENERAL MILLS
(K) KELLOGG'S
(P) POST
(Q) QUAKER OATS

PERIODIC BREAKFAST TABLE
Magazine page (detail)
Designer: Catherine Weese
Photography: John Halpern
Publisher: Patsy Tarr,
2wice Magazine

This chart organizes breakfast cereals by shape and annotates them according to a dozen characteristics, from fiber content to price per pound. Visual displays of data allow readers to quickly compare items. One might observe, for example, that in breakfast cereals, intensity of sugar is usually accompanied by intensity of color.

Train No.	3701	XM 3301	3801	A 67	3 3803	3 3201	A3 51	.3 3703	3 3807	3 3203	A3 61	3 3809	A3 47	3 3901	3 3811	3 3903	3 3813	3205	3815	3817	3819	3207	3821	3823	3825	.3209	3827	3829	3831
	A.M.	A.M	A.M	A.M	A.M	A.M	A.M	A.M	A.M	A.M	A.M	A.M	A.M	A.M	A.M	A.M	A.M	A.M	A.M	A.M	A.M	A.M	A.M	A.M	A.M	A.M	P.M	P.M	P.M
New York, N.Y.	12.10	12.40	1.30	3.52	4.50	6.10	6.25	6.35	6.50	7.10	7.30	7.33	7.45	7.50	8.05	8.25	8.40	8.50	9.10	9.40	10.10	10.25	10.40	11.10	11.40	11.50	12.10	12.40	1.10
Newark, N.J. P	12.24	12.55	1.44	4.07	5.04	6.24	6.38	6.49	7.04	7.24	7.45	7.47	7.59	8.04	8.19	8.39	8.54	9.04	9.24	9.54	10.24	10.39	10.54	11.24	11.54	12.04	12.24	12.54	1.24
North Elizabeth										7.30				8.10															
Elizabeth	12.31	1.03	1.51		5.11	6.31		6.56	7.11	7.32		7.54		8.13	8.26	8.46	9.01	9.11	9.31	10.01	10.31	10.46	11.01	11.31	12.01	12.11	12.31	1.01	1.31
Linden	12.36		1.56		5.16	6.36		7.01	7.15	7.37		7.59		8.18	8.31	8.51	9.06		9.36	10.06	10.36		11.06	11.36	12.06		12.36	1.06	1.36
North Rahway								7.03		7.39				8.20	8.33	8.54													
Rahway	12.40	1.11	2.00		5.20	6.40		7.06	7.20	7.42		8.03		8.24	8.36	8.57	9.10	9.18	9.40	10.10	10.40	10.53	11.10	11.40	12.10	12.18	12.40	1.10	1.40
Metro Park (Iselin)	12.44		2.04	4.26	5.24		6.56	7.10	7.25		8.04	8.07	8.15		8.40		9.14		9.44	10.14	10.44		11.14	11.44	12.14		12.44	1.14	1.44
Metuchen	12.48		2.08		5.28			7.14	7.29			8.11			8.44		9.18		9.48	10.18	10.48		11.18	11.48	12.18		12.48	1.18	1.48
Edison	12.51		2.11					7.17	7.32			8.14			8.47		9.21			10.21			11.21		12.21			1.21	
New Brunswick	12.55		2.15		5.35		7.05	7.21	7.35			8.18	8.25		8.50		9.25		9.54	10.25	10.54		11.25	11.54	12.25		12.54	1.25	1.54
Jersey Avenue	1.02		2.18					7.28				8.21					9.28			10.28			11.28		12.28			1.28	
Princeton Jct. S			2.31		5.50		7.19		7.50			8.34	8.41		9.05		9.41		10.09	10.41	11.09		11.41	12.09	12.41		1.09	1.41	2.09
Trenton, N.J.			2.42	4.58	6.03		7.28		8.01		8.31	8.44	8.52		9.16		9.52		10.19	10.52	11.19		11.52	12.19	12.52		1.22	1.52	2.20

am ⊕

New York, NY	12.10	12.40	1.30	3.52	4.50	6.10	6.25	6.35	6.50	7.10	7.30	7.33	7.45	7.50	8.05	8.25	8.40	8.50	9.10		9.40	10.10		10.25	10.40	11.10	11.40		
Newark, NJ P	12.24	12.55	1.44	4.07	5.04	6.24	6.38	6.49	7.04	7.24	7.45	7.47	7.59	8.04	8.19	8.39	8.54	9.04	9.24		9.54	10.24		10.39	10.54	11.24	11.54		
North Elizabeth											7.30				8.10														
Elizabeth	12.31	1.03	1.51	. .	5.11	6.31	. .	6.56	7.11	7.32		7.54		8.13	8.26	8.46	9.01	9.11	9.31		10.01	10.31		10.46	11.01	11.31	12.01		
Linden	12.36		1.56		5.16	6.36		7.01	7.15	7.37		7.59		8.18	8.31	8.51	9.06		9.36		10.06	10.36		. .	11.06	11.36	12.06		
North Rahway								7.03		7.39				8.20	8.33	8.54													
Rahway	12.40	1.11	2.00		5.20	6.40		7.06	7.20	7.42		8.03		8.24	8.36	8.57	9.10	9.18	9.40		10.10	10.40		10.53	11.10	11.40	12.10		
Metro Park (Iselin)	12.44		2.04	4.26	5.24		6.56	7.10	7.25		8.04	8.07	8.15		8.40		9.14		9.44		10.14	10.44			11.14	11.44	12.14		
Metuchen	12.48		2.08	. .	5.28			7.14	7.29			8.11	. .		8.44		9.18		9.48		10.18	10.48			11.18	11.48	12.16		
Edison	12.51		2.11	. .	. .			7.17	7.32			8.14	. .		8.47		9.21		. .		10.21				11.21		12.21		
New Brunswick	12.55		2.15	. .	5.35		7.05	7.21	7.35			8.18	8.25		8.50		9.25		9.54		10.25	10.54			11.25	11.54	12.25		
Jersey Avenue	1.02		2.18	. .	. .			7.28				8.21	. .		. .		9.28				10.28				11.28		12.28		
Princeton Junction S			2.31		5.50		7.19		7.50			8.34	8.41		9.05		9.41		10.09		10.41	11.09			11.41	12.09	12.41		
Trenton, NJ			2.42	4.58	6.03		7.28		8.01		8.31	8.44	8.52		9.16		9.52		10.19		10.52	11.19			11.52	12.19	12.52		
TRAIN NUMBER	3701	3301	3801	67	3803	3201	51	3703	3807	3203	61	3809	47	3901	3811	3903	3813	3205	3815	3817	3819	3207	3821	3823	3825				
NOTES		XM		⊷	3	3	⊷3	3	3	3	⊷3	3	⊷3	3	3	3	3												

NEW JERSEY TRANSIT, NORTHEASTERN CORRIDOR TIMETABLE
Original schedule with redesign by Edward Tufte
From Edward Tufte, *Envisioning Information* (Cheshire, Conn.: Graphics Press, 1990).
The original design (top) is organized with heavy horizontal and vertical divisions. Tufte calls this a "data prison." His redesign uses the alignment of the typographic elements themselves to express the table's underlying structure.

ACCOUNT	ACCOUNT NAME	TOTAL FOR ACCO
101001	Instructional Supplies	$3,65
101002	Office Supplies	$46
102004	Equipment - Non-Capital	$1,28
105009	Travel-Conference Fees	$56
110004	Miscellaneous Entertainment	$8
114006	Postage/Shipping-Local Courier	$21
151108	Temp Staff-Contractual	$7
151181	Honoraria-Critics/Vis Artist	$1,00
	DEPARTMENTAL EXPENDITURES	$7,35

The design of charts and graphs is a rich and subtle area of typographic practice. In a data table, the grid acquires semantic significance. Designers (and software defaults) often over-emphasize the grid, rather than allowing the data to command the page and stake out its own territory.

TYPE CRIME:

DATA PRISON
The rules and boxes used in data tables should illuminate the relationships among data, not trap each entry inside a heavily guarded cell.

118   BEHAVIOUR TO INTOXICATED FRIENDS.

Tabular View.—Experiments on Ants under Chloroform and Intoxicated.

	FRIENDS			STRANGERS		
	To Nest	To Water	Unremoved	To Nest	To Water	Unremoved
CHLOROFORMED ANTS.						
Sept. 10	...	...	4	...	4	...
14	...	4	...	2 and brought out again	2	...
15	1 and brought out again	1	...	...	2	2
29	...	5	...	...	4	...
Oct. 2	...	5	...	1 and brought out again	4	...
6	...	5	...	...	4	...
	1	20	4	3	20	2
INTOXICATED ANTS.						
Nov. 20	3	2	...	...	5	1
22	2	...	2	...	8	...
In these cases some of the Ants had partly recovered; in the following they were quite insensible.						
Dec. 1	7 none brought out again	2	...	3 all these brought out again	6	...
8	16 none brought out again	5	...	3 all these brought out again	15	...
Jan. 15	...	...	4	...	3	1
17	4 none brought out again	...	...	3 one brought out again	6	...
	27	7	4	2	30	1

INTOXICATED FRIENDS
Data table from Sir John Lubbock, *Ants, Bees, and Wasps* (New York: D. Appleton and Company, 1893). *The author of this experiment studied how ants responded upon meeting either "friends" (members of their own colony) or "strangers." In the first experiment, the friends and strangers were rendered unconscious with chloroform. In the second experiment, the ants were merely intoxicated. The chloroformed ants—whether friends or strangers—were usually taken for dead and pitched into a moat of water surrounding the colony. The intoxicated ants were treated with more discrimination. Many of the drunken friends were taken back to the nest for care and rehabilitation, whereas drunken strangers were generally tossed into the moat. Ants, one might conclude, should not rely on the kindness of strangers.*

CHLOROFORMED ANTS

	FRIENDS				STRANGERS			
	LEFT ALONE	TAKEN TO NEST	THROWN IN WATER	BOTH NEST AND WATER	LEFT ALONE	TAKEN TO NEST	THROWN IN WATER	BOTH NEST AND WATER
SEPT 10	••••						••••	
14			••••			••	••	••
15			•	•	••		••	
29			•••••				••••	
OCT 02			•••••				••••	•
06			•••••				••••	
TOTAL	04		20	01	02		20	03

INTOXICATED ANTS

	FRIENDS				STRANGERS			
	LEFT ALONE	TAKEN TO NEST	THROWN IN WATER	BOTH NEST AND WATER	LEFT ALONE	TAKEN TO NEST	THROWN IN WATER	BOTH NEST AND WATER
NOV 20		•••	••		•		•••••	
22	••	••					••••••••	
DEC 01		•••••••	••				••••••	•••
05		••••••••••••••	•••••				••••••••••••	•••
JAN 15	••••				•		•••	
17		••••				••	••••••	•
TOTAL	06	32	09		02	02	43	07

Find a chart from an old science book or other source, and redesign it. Shown at left is a nineteenth-century table documenting an experiment about ants. The old design emphasizes vertical divisions at the expense of horizontal ones, and it jumbles together text and numbers within the table cells.

The redesign (above) eliminates many of the ruled lines, replacing them, where needed, with a pale tone that unifies the long horizontal rows of data. The redesigned chart also replaces most of the numerals with dots, a technique that lets the eye visually compare the results without having to read each numeral separately.

www.typotheque.com

[fonts]
[other products]
[licensing]
[type utilities]
[articles]
[discussion]
[about]

search ?

Typotheque is a type foundry developing and marketing contemporary original fonts for the Mac and PC. Our commitment is to continue the traditions of independent type foundries, contributing our tiny bit to the continuous sequence of type history, creating quality typefaces that reflect our time and serve its needs.

Latest updates:
—Fedra Sans 2.0 released (16 Jul 2003)
—Fedra reviewed by Andy Crewdson (16 Jul 2003)
—*Letterletter* by Gerrit Noordzij with a 30% discount (09 Jul 2003)
—*The Elements of Typographic Style* now available (06 Jul 2003)
—*A Short History of the Printed Word* now available (06 Jul 2003)
—*Jigsaw* out (18 Jun 2003)

Add yourself to our news email list. We use the list to help keep you informed of the new fonts, special limited offers, and major updates. We never sell your email. (You will receive 3-4 emails a year)

your e-mail here   send

© 1999-2003

Fedra Sans 2.0

Light **Book** Normal **Medium Bold**

Version 2.0 of Fedra Sans improves the consistency of the font and adds new versions to the type family. Details of the revision are explained in this PDF file.

The articles section is our attempt to collect relevant published and previously unpublished texts, not directed exclusively to academic peers and students, but to a broader audience of individuals with an interest in design criticism, typography and graphic design. At the moment the collection contains over 80 texts in four categories: features, reviews, interviews and essays.

A

Try our interactive Font Tester with memory. You can preview and try our complete library of fonts, as well as chat with your friends. Works also with special characters and characters with diacritics.

❶ЕВГЕ2003

Fedra Serif Greek won the first prize at this year's Greek Graphic Design & Illustration Awards. Both monotonic and polytonic versions are coming soon.

Examples of Typotheque fonts in use.

Besides fonts, we offer a small selection of books on type design and typography.

TYPOTHEQUE.COM
Web site, 2003
Designer: Peter Bilak
Multi-column grids provide a logical way to organize Web pages. Content occupies the center; the top and left "margins" are reserved for branding and navigation.

STRIKE!

House-a-Rama Font Kit: $100

- Three Fonts
- 54 Dingbats
- 14 Illustrations
- Four Patterns

BUY IT NOW!

HOUSEIND.COM
Web site, 2004
Designes: Andy Cruz. Tal
Leming, Ken Barber, Rich
Roat, and Bondé Prang
Publisher: House Industries
*Like many Web sites, this one
places local navigation in the left
column and reserves space for
branding and global navigation
across the top. These components
serve as a frame for the content
at the center.*

AIGA: JAMBALAYA
Poster, 1997
Designer: Stefan Sagmeister
Publisher: American Institute
of Graphic Arts
*Letters can be made from
nearly anything, even chicken feet.*

APPENDIX

Helpful hints, dire warnings,
and other resources

These interruptions—especially the snide remarks--are driving me crazy.

CRIME: *Two hyphens in place of em dash*

Dashes express a break in the flow of a sentence. In a word-processed document, dashes can be indicated with two hyphens. Em dashes are required, however, in typesetting. No spaces are used around dashes.

El Lissitzky lived 1890–1941. Rodchenko lived longer (1891-1956).

CRIME: *Hyphen between numbers*

An en dash connects two numbers. It means "up to and including," not "between." No spaces are used around en dashes.

It's okay to be second-best, but never, ever second–best.

CRIME: *En dash in hyphenated word*

Do not use en dashes where the humble hyphen is required.

In the beginning was…the word….Typography came later.

An ellipsis character is used here in place of separate points.

The periods in an ellipsis can be separated with word spaces, or, as we prefer, they can be tracked open (letterspaced). Most typefaces include an ellipsis character, whose points are more tightly spaced. After a sentence, use a period plus an ellipsis (four dots).

She was 5'2" with eyes of blue. "I'm not dumb," she said. "I'm prime."

CRIME: *Prime marks (a.k.a. dumb quotes) used in place of quotation marks*

The purpose of prime marks, or hatch marks, is to indicate inches and feet. Their use to mark quotations is a common blight across the typographic landscape.

"I'm not smart," he replied. "I'm a quotation mark."

Unlike prime marks, quotation marks include an opening and closing character. Single close quotes also serve as apostrophes. Incorrectly used prime marks must be routed out and destroyed.

Don't put two spaces between sentences. They leave an ugly gap.

CRIME: *Two spaces between sentences*

Although writers persist in putting double spaces between sentences (a habit often learned in high school), all such spaces must be purged from a manuscript when it is set in type.

DASHES Dashes of different length have specific uses that every designer must learn. Writers or clients often supply manuscripts that employ incorrect dashes or use substitute characters.

EM DASHES express strong grammatical breaks. An em dash is one-em wide—the width of the point size of the typeface. In manuscripts, dashes are often represented with a double hyphen (--); these must be replaced.

EN DASHES serve primarily to connect numbers (1–10). An en is half the width of an em. Manuscripts rarely employ en dashes, so the designer needs to supply them.

HYPHENS connect linked words and phrases, and they break words at the ends of lines. Typesetting programs break words automatically. Disable auto hyphenation when working with ragged or centered text; use discretionary hyphens instead, and only when unavoidable.

DISCRETIONARY HYPHENS, which are inserted manually to break lines, only appear in the document if they are needed. (If a text is reflowed in subsequent editing, a discretionary hyphen will disappear.) Wayward hyphens often occur in the mid-dle of a line when the typesetter has inserted a "hard" hyphen instead of a discretionary one.

PUNCTUATION Consult a definitive work such as The Chicago Manual of Style for complete rules of punctuation. The following are especially pertinent for typographers.

QUOTATION MARKS have distinct "open" and "closed" forms, unlike "hatch marks," which are straight up and down. A single close quote also serves as an apostrophe ("It's Bob's font."). Hatch marks should only be used to indicate inches and feet (5'2"). Used incorrectly, hatches are known as "dumb quotes." Although computer operating systems and typesetting programs often include automatic "smart quote" features, e-mailed, word-processed, and/or client-supplied text can be riddled with dumb quotes. Auto smart quote programs often render apostrophes upside down ('tis instead of 'tis), so designers must be vigilant and learn the necessary keystrokes.

ELLIPSES consist of three periods, which can be rendered with no spaces between them, or with open tracking (letterspacing), or with word spaces. An ellipsis indicates an omitted section in a quoted text or...a temporal break. Most typefaces include an ellipsis character, which presents closely spaced points.

WORD SPACES are created by the space bar. Use just one space between sentences or after a comma, colon, or semicolon. One of the first steps in typesetting a manuscript is to purge it of all double spaces. Thus the space bar should not be used to create indents or otherwise position text on a line. Use tabs instead. HTML refuses to recognize double spaces altogether.

EN SPACES are wider than word spaces. An en space can be used to render a more emphatic distance between elements on a line: for example, to separate a subhead from the text that immediately follows, or to separate elements gathered along a single line in a letterhead.

The keystrokes listed below are commonly used in word processing, page layout, and illustration software. Keystrokes will vary in some applications. (These work for Quark XPress and InDesign.) Some fonts do not include a full range of special characters.

DASHES	keystrokes (Mac)
— em-dash	shift-option-hyphen
– en-dash	option-hyphen
- standard hyphen	(hyphen key)
- discretionary hyphen	command-hyphen

PUNCTUATION	keystrokes (Mac)
' single open quote	option-]
' single close quote	shift-option-]
" double open quote	option-[
" double close quote	shift-option-[
ellipsis	option-;

OTHER MARKS	keystrokes (Mac)
( ) en space	option-space bar
† dagger	option-t
‡ double dagger	shift-option-7
© copyright symbol	option-g
® resister symbol	option-r
ff ff ligature	shift-option-2
fi fi ligature	shift-option-5
fl fl ligature	shift-option-6
é *accent aigu*	option-e + e
è *accent grave*	option-` + e
à *accent grave*	option-` + a
ù *accent grave*	option-` + u
ç *cédille*	option-c
ü *umlaut*	option-u + u
ö *umlaut*	option-u + o

Only an editor can see beyond a writer's navel.

No matter how brilliant your prose, an editor will discover errors in spelling, grammar, consistency, redundancy, and construction.

Writers should not over-format their texts.

The time you spend fiddling with formatting will be spent again by the editor and/or designer, removing extra keystrokes. Provide flush left copy, in one font, double-spaced.

Some lessons learned in high school are best forgotten.

One of them is dotting your i's with hearts and smiley faces. The other is leaving two spaces between sentences. In typesetting, one space only must be left between sentences.

The space bar is not a design tool.

Don't use the space bar to create indents (just key in a single tab), and don't use extra spaces to create centered effects or layouts (unless you really are e. e. cummings).

Every change threatens to introduce new errors.

Each time a file is "corrected" new errors can appear, from problems with rags, justification, and page breaks to spelling mistakes, missing words, and botched or incomplete corrections.

Don't wait for the proofs to seriously examine the typeset text.

Changes made after a printer's proof has been made (blue line, press proof, or other) are expensive. They also will slow down your project, which, of course, is already late.

Famous last words: "We'll catch it in the blue lines."

EDITORS Since the onslaught of desktop publishing back in the dark days of the mid-1980s, graphic designers have taken on roles formerly occupied by distinct trades, such as typesetting and mechanical pasteup. Designers are often expected to be editors as well. Every project should have a true editor, a person with the training and disposition to judge the correctness, accuracy, and consistency of written content. Neither a project's author nor its designer should be its editor, who is rightly a neutral party between them. If a project team includes no properly trained editor, try to find one. If that fails, make sure that *someone* is responsible for this crucial role, for the failure to edit carefully is the source of costly and embarrassing errors.

Editing a text for publication has three basic phases. *Developmental editing* addresses broad issues of the content and the structure of a work; indeed, it can include judging a work's fitness for publication in the first place. *Copy editing* (also called line editing or manuscript editing) seeks to root out redundancies, inconsistencies, grammatical errors, and other flaws appearing across the body of the work. The copy editor—who must study every word and sentence—is not expected to question the overall meaning or structure of a work, nor to alter an author's style, but rather to refine and correct. *Proofreading*, which checks the correctness, consistency, and flow of designed, typeset pages, is the final stage. Depending on the nature of the project and its team, each of these phases may go through several rounds.

ANATOMY OF AN ERROR After a document has been written, edited, designed, and proofread, a printer's proof is created by the printer from the digital files supplied by the designer. At this point, making changes is expensive. Many clients (or authors) fail to recognize errors (or make decisions) until the printer's proofs are issued. This luxury has its costs, and someone will have to pay.

PE'S (PRINTER'S ERRORS) These are errors that can be assigned to the printer, and they must be corrected at no expense to the designer or client. A printer's error is an obvious and blatant divergence from the digital files and other instructions provided by the designer and agreed to by the printer. Printer's errors are surprisingly rare in the digital age.

AA'S (AUTHOR'S ALTERATIONS) These are not so rare. Author's alterations are changes to the approved text or layout of the work. If the change originates with the designer, the designer is responsible. If it originates with the client or author, she or he is responsible. Keeping records of each phase of a project's development is helpful in assigning blame later. Designers can charge the client a fee for the AA on top of the printer's fee, as the designer must correct the file, print out new hard copy, get the client's approval (again), communicate with the printer (again), and so on. If agreed to in advance, designers can charge AA fees for *any* change to an approved document, even before the printer's proof is issued.

EA'S (EDITOR'S ALTERATIONS) Errors made by the editor are the responsibility of the editor's employer, typically the client or publisher of the work. Good editors help prevent everyone's errors from occurring in the first place.

For more detailed information about the editorial process, see *The Chicago Manual of Style, 15th Edition* (Chicago: University of Chicago Press, 2003).

Manuscript editing, also called copyediting or line editing, requires attention to every word in a manuscript, a thorough knowledge of the style to be followed, and the ability to make quick, logical, and defensible decisions. *The Chicago Manual of Style, 2003*

~~delete~~
DELETE

pose trans
TRANSPOSE

~~let it stand~~
STET ("LET IT STAND")

add#space
SEPARATE; ADD SPACE

second=rate
ADD HYPHEN

left◠over
REMOVE HYPHEN

Dashing-no?
EM DASH (—)

1914-1918
EN DASH (–)

italic
ITALIC

boldface
BOLDFACE

remove underline
REMOVE UNDERLINE

case
LOWERCASE

case
UPPERCASE

case
SMALL CAPS

Writers, editors, and designers use special symbols to mark changes such as ~~deleting~~, posing trans, or ~~correcting~~ substituting words or phrases. If you change your mind about a ~~deletion~~, place dots beneath it. Remove a comma by circling it. Add a period with a circled dot. If two words run together, insert a straight line and a space mark.

To combine two paragraphs, connect them with a line and note the comment "run-in" in the margin. (Circling notes prevents the typesetter from confusing comments with content.)

Insert two short lines to hyphenate a word such as secondrate. When removing a hyphen, close up the leftover space. To replace a hyphen with an em dash-a symbol that expresses a grammatical break-write a tiny M above the hyphen. If a manuscript indicates dashes with double hyphens--like this-- the typesetter or designer is expected to convert them without being told. Use an en dash, not a hyphen, to connect two numbers, such as 1914-1918.

In addition to correcting grammar, spelling, punctuation, and clarity of prose, editors indicate typographic styles such as italic (with an underscore) and boldface (with a wavy line). Underlining, which is rarely used in formal typography, is removed like this. Draw A Line Through A Capital Letter to change it to lowercase. underline a letter with three strokes to capitalize it. Use two underlines to indicate small capitals.

Double-space the manuscript and leave a generous margin to provide room for comments and corrections. Align the text flush left, ragged right, and disable automatic hyphenation.

Don't mark manuscripts or proofs with Post-It notes. They can fall off, block the text, and make the document hard to photocopy.

Editing an electronic file and allowing the author to see the changes is called *redlining* (also referred to as "editing online"). Basic housekeeping includes removing all double spaces and converting hatches (a.ka. "dumb quotes") to quotation marks and apostrophes (a.k.a. "smart quotes"). The editor need not point out these changes to the author.

Changes to the structure and wording of the text must be communicated to the author. A visual convention is needed for showing ~~deleted~~ and added material. ~~Words to be removed~~ are typically struck out, and words added or substituted can be underlined, highlighted, or rendered in color. A line in the margin indicates that a change has been recommended. [Queries to the author are set off with brackets.][A]

Underlining, or striking out, punctuation is visually confusing, so the editor often strikes out an entire word~~, or phrase,~~ —or phrase—and types in the freshly punctuated passage as an addition. To hyphenate a word such as ~~secondrate~~ *second-rate*, strike it out and add the hyphenated form. When converting hyphens to en dashes (1914–18)—or changing double hyphens to em dashes—the editor simply keys them in. Typographic styles such as *italic*, **boldface**, and SMALL CAPITALS can also be changed directly.

Although redlining is wonderfully fluid and direct, it can be dangerous. The editor must scrupulously remove all traces of the editing process before releasing the file for design and typesetting. Potential disasters include words that are stucktogether, a missing , or a forgotten comment to the author [Are you nuts?].

A. Queries to the author can also take the form of footnotes. Identify these notes with letters, so they are not confused with footnotes that belong to the text.

EDITORIAL CHANGE	MARK IN TEXT	MARK IN MARGIN	EDITORIAL CHANGE	MARK IN TEXT	MARK IN MARGIN
delete	~~delete~~	℘	letterspace	(LETTERSPACE)	(ls)
delete and close up	delete and close up	℘	close up	clo se up	⌒
let it stand (stet)	~~let it stand~~	(stet)	insert space	insert#space	#
insert text or character	insert ∧	text	reduce space	reduce /space	less #
run in paragraph	run in / paragraph	(run in)	transpose	pose⌐trans⌐	(tr)
start new paragraph	start new paragraph	¶	flush right	⌐ flush right	(fr)
insert punctuation	insert ∧ punctuation	⌃⁄	flush left	⌐ flush left	(fl)
change punctuation	change, punctuation	?/	indent 1 em	☐ indent 1 em	☐
insert hyphen	insert hyphen ∧	=	move to next line	move to next ⌐line	(T.O.)
insert parentheses	insert ∧ parentheses ∧	(/)	superscript	superscript1⌄	⌄1
insert en or em dash	insert en dash ∧	N̲ M̲	align vertically	‖ align vertically	‖
insert quotes	insert quotes ∧ ∧	⁶⁶⌄ ⌄	align horizontally	align horizontal	═
capitalize	capitalize	(cap)	spell out abbreviation	spell out (abbrev.)	(sp)
change to lowercase	LOWERCASE	(lc)	use ligature	use ligature (flour)	⌒fl
change to small caps	small caps	(sc)	query that cannot be resolved by proofreader	(query)	(?)
change to bold	bold	(bf)			
change to roman	(roman)	(rom)			
wrong font	wrong (font)	(wf)			

Proofreader's marks derived from The Chicago Manual of Style *and David Jury,* About Face: Reviving the Rules of Typography *(East Sussex: Rotovision, 2001). Marking conventions do vary slightly from source to source.*

PROOFREADING takes place *after* an edited manuscript has been designed and typeset. New errors can appear at any time during the handling of a document, and old errors previously unrecognized—can leap to the eye once the text has been set in type. The proofreader corrects gross errors in spelling, grammar, and fact, but avoid changes in style and content. Changes at this stage are not only expensive but they can affect the page design and introduce new problems.

Proofreading is different task from editing, although the editor may play a role in it, along with or in addition to the author or client. Although the *designer or typesetter*[1] should not be given the role of proof reader, designers must nonetheless inspect their work carefully for errors before sending it back to the editor, author, or client.

Mark all corrections in the margin of the proof, and indicate the position of changes within the text. Don't write between the lines. Many of the same interline symbols are used in proofreading and in copy editing, but proofreaders use an additional set of flags for marginal notes.

Don't obliterate what is being crossed out and deleted so the typesetter can read it.

Mark all changes on one master proof. If several copies of the proof are circulated for approval, one person (usually the editor) is responsible for transferring corrections to a master copy.

Don't give the designer a proof with conflicting or indecisive comments.

TYPES OF *proofs* Depending on how a project is organized and produced, some or all of the following proofs may be involved.

Galley proofs are typically supplied in a book-length project. They consist of text that has been typeset but not paginated and do not yet include illustrations.

Page proofs are broken into pages and include illustrations, page numbers, running heads, and other details.

Revised proofs include changes that have been recommended by the proofreader and input by the designer or typesetter.

Printer's proofs are generated by the printer. At this phase, changes become increasingly costly, complex, and ill-advised. In theory, one is only looking for printers' errors—not errors in design or verbal style—at this stage. Printer's proofs might include blue lines (one color only) and/or color proofs.

---

1. The designer and typesetter may be the same person. In a design studio, as opposed to a publishing house, designers are generally responsible for typesetting.

Think more, design less.

Many desperate acts of design (including gradients, drop shadows, and the gratuitous use of transparency) are perpetrated in the absence of a strong concept. A good idea provides a framework for design decisions, guiding the work.

Say more, write less.

Just as designers should avoid filling up space with arbitrary visual effects, writers should remember that no one loves their words as much as they do.

Spend more, buy less.

Cheap stuff is usually cheap because of how it's made, what it's made of, and who made it. Buy better quality goods, less often.

May your thoughts be deep and your wounds be shallow.

Always work with a sharp blade. Although graphic design is not a terribly dangerous occupation, many late-night accidents occur involving dull X-Acto blades. Protect your printouts from senseless bloodshed.

Density is the new white space.

In an era of exurban sprawl, closely knit neighborhoods have renewed appeal. So, too, on page and screen, where a rich texture of information can function better than sparseness and isolation.

Make the shoe fit, not the foot.

Rather than force content into rigid containers, create systems that are flexible and responsive to the material they are intended to accommodate.

Make it bigger. *(Courtesy of Paula Scher)*

Amateur typographers make their type too big. The 12-point default—which looks okay on the screen—often looks horsey on the page. Experienced designers, however, make their type too tiny: shown here, 7.5 point Scala.

It is easier to talk than to listen.

Pay attention to your clients, your users, your readers, and your friends. Your design will get better as you listen to other people.

Design is an art of situations.

Designers respond to a need, a problem, a circumstance, that arises in the world. The best work is produced in relation to interesting situations—an open-minded client, a good cause, or great content.

No job is too small.

A graphic designer can set out to change the world one business card at a time— as long as it is the business card of a really interesting person.

An interface calls attention to itself at its point of failure.

Design helps the systems of daily life run smoothly, letting users and readers ignore how things are put together. Design should sometimes announce itself in order to shed light on the system, exposing its construction, identity, personality, and politics.

The idea is the machine that makes the art. *(Courtesy of Sol Lewitt)*

A powerful concept can drive decisions about color, layout, type choice, format, and so on, preventing senseless acts of whimsy. (On the other hand, senseless acts of whimsy sometimes lead to powerful concepts.)

The early bird gets to work before everyone else.

Your best time for thinking could be early in the morning, late at night, or even, in rare circumstances, during class or between nine and five. Whether your best time is in the shower, at the gym, or on the train, use it for your hardest thinking.

Build the discourse.

Design is social. It lives in society, it creates society, and it needs a society of its own— a community of designers committed to advancing and debating our shared hopes and desires. Read, write, and talk about design whenever you can.

Go forth and reproduce.

LETTER

Bartram, Alan. *Five Hundred Years of Book Design*. London: British Library, 2001.

Blackwell, Lewis. *Twentieth-Century Type*. New Haven: Yale University Press, 2004.

Boyarski, Dan, and Christine Neuwirth, Jodi Forlizzi, and Susan Harkness Regli. "A Study of Fonts Designed for Screen Display." *CHI 98* (April 1998): 18–23.

Broos, Kees, and Paul Hefting. *Dutch Graphic Design: A Century*. Cambridge: MIT Press, 1993.

Burke, Christopher. *Paul Renner: The Art of Typography*. New York: Princeton Architectural Press, 1998.

Christin, Anne-Marie. *A History of Writing, from Hieroglyph to Multimedia*. Paris: Flammarion, 2002.

Crouwel, Wim. *New Alphabet: An Introduction for a Programmed Typography*. Amsterdam: Wim Crouwel/Total Design, 1967.

———, Kees Broos, and David Quay. *Wim Crouwel: Alphabets*. Amsterdam: BIS Publishers, 2003.

Cruz, Andy, Ken Barber, and Rich Roat. *House Industries*. Berlin: Die Gestalten Verlag, 2004.

Eason, Ron, and Sarah Rookledge. *Rookledge's International Directory of Type Designers: A Biographical Handbook*. New York: Sarabande Press, 1994.

Gray, Nicolete. *A History of Lettering*. Oxford: Phaidon Press, 1986.

Heller, Steven, and Philip B. Meggs, eds. *Texts on Type: Critical Writings on Typography*. New York: Allworth Press, 2001.

Hornung, Clarence. *Handbook of Early Advertising Art*. New York: Dover Publications, 1956.

Johnston, Edward. *Writing & Illuminating & Lettering*. London: Sir Isaac Pitman & Sons, 1932.

Kelly, Rob Roy. *American Wood Type: 1828–1900*. New York: Da Capo Press, 1969.

Kinross, Robin. *Unjustified Texts: Perspectives on Typography*. London: Hyphen Press, 2002.

Lawson, Alexander. *Anatomy of a Typeface*. Boston: David R. Godine, 1990.

Lewis, John. *Anatomy of Printing: The Influences of Art and History on its Design*. New York: Watson-Guptill Publications, 1970.

———. *Typography: Basic Principles, Influences and Trends Since the Nineteenth Century*. New York: Reinhold Publishing, 1963.

McMurtrie, Douglas. *The Book: The Story of Printing and Bookmaking*. New York: Dorset Press, 1943.

Morison, Stanley. *Letter Forms*. London: Nattali & Maurice, 1968.

Noordzij, Gerrit. *Letterletter: An Inconsistent Collection of Tentative Theories That Do Not Claim Any Authority Other Than That of Common Sense*. Vancouver: Hartley and Marks, 2000.

Pardoe, F. E. *John Baskerville of Birmingham: Letter-Founder and Printer*. London: Frederick Muller Limited, 1975.

Shelley, Mary. *Frankenstein*. New York: The Modern Library, 1999. First published 1831.

Re, Margaret. *Typographically Speaking: The Art of Matthew Carter*. New York: Princeton Architectural Press, 2002.

Updike, Daniel. *Printing Types: Their History, Forms, and Use, Volumes I and II*. New York: Dover Publications, 1980.

VanderLans, Rudy, and Zuzana Licko. *Emigre: Graphic Design into the Digital Realm*. New York: Van Nostrand Reinhold, 1993.

TEXT

Barthes, Roland. *Image/Music/Text*. Trans. Stephen Heath. New York: Hill and Wang, 1977.

Baudrillard, Jean. *For a Critique of the Political Economy of the Sign*. St. Louis, Mo.: Telos Press, 1981.

Benjamin, Walter. *Reflections*. Ed. Peter Demetz. New York: Schocken Books, 1978.

Bolter, Jay David. *Writing Space: Computers, Hypertext, and the Remediation of Print*. Mahwah, N. J.: Lawrence Erlbaum Associates, 2001.

Derrida, Jacques. *Of Grammatology*. Trans. Gayatri Chakravorty Spivak. Baltimore: Johns Hopkins University Press, 1976.

Diamond, Jared. *Guns, Germs, and Steel: The Fates of Human Societies*. New York: W. W. Norton, 1997.

Kaplan, Nancy. "Blake's Problem and Ours: Some Reflections on the Image and the Word." *Readerly/Writerly Texts*, 3.2 (Spring/Summer 1996), 115–33.

Gould, John D. *et al.* "Reading from CRT Displays Can Be as Fast as Reading from Paper." *Human Factors* 29, 5 (1987): 497–517.

Helfand, Jessica. *Screen: Essays on Graphic Design, New Media, and Visual Culture*. New York: Princeton Architectural Press, 2001.

Lessig, Lawrence. *Free Culture: How Big Media Uses Technology and the Law to Lock Down Culture and Control Creativity*. New York: Penguin, 2004.

Laurel, Brenda. *Utopian Entrepreneur*. Cambridge: MIT Press, 2001.

Lunenfeld, Peter. *Snap to Grid: A User's Guide to Digital Arts, Media, and Cultures*. Cambridge: MIT Press, 2001.

Manovich, Lev. *The Language of New Media*. Cambridge: MIT Press, 2002.

McCoy, Katherine and Michael McCoy. *Cranbrook Design: The New Discourse*. New York: Rizzoli, 1990.

———. "American Graphic Design Expression." *Design Quarterly* 148 (1990): 4–22.

McLuhan, Marshall. *The Gutenberg Galaxy*. Toronto: University of Toronto Press, 1962.

Moulthrop, Stuart. "You Say You Want a Revolution? Hypertext and the Laws of Media." *The New Media Reader*. Noah Wardrip-Fruin and Nick Monfort, eds. Cambridge, Mass.: MIT Press, 2003. 691–703.

Nielsen, Jakob. *Designing Web Usability*. Indianapolis: New Riders, 2000.

Ong, Walter. *Orality and Literacy: The Technologizing of the Word*. New York: Methuen, 1982.

Raskin, Jef. *The Human Interface: New Directions for Designing Interactive Systems*. Reading, Mass.: Addison-Wesley, 2000.

Ronell, Avital. *The Telephone Book: Technology, Schizophrenia, Electric Speech*. Lincoln: University of Nebraska Press, 1989.

GRID

Berners-Lee, Tim. *Weaving the Web: The Original Design and Ultimate Destiny of the World Wide Web.* New York: HarperCollins, 1999.

Bosshard, Hans Rudolf. *Der Typografische Raster/The Typographic Grid.* Sulgen, Switzerland: Verlag Niggli, 2000.

Cantz, Hatje. *Karl Gerstner: Review of 5 x 10 Years of Graphic Design etc.* Ostfildern-Ruit, Germany: Hatje Cantz Verlag, 2001.

Elam, Kimberly. *Geometry of Design.* New York: Princeton Architectural Press, 2001.

Gerstner, Karl. *Designing Programmes.* Switzerland: Arthur Niggli Ltd., 1964.

William Gibson. *Neuromancer.* New York: Ace Books, 1984.

Hochuli, Jost, and Robin Kinross. *Designing Books: Practice and Theory.* London: Hyphen Press, 1996.

Jute, André. *Grids: The Structure of Graphic Design.* Switzerland: RotoVision, 1996.

Krauss, Rosalind. "Grids." *The Originality of the Avant-Garde and Other Modernist Myths.* Cambridge: MIT Press, 1985. 9–22.

Kusters, Christian and Emily King. *Restart: New Systems in Graphic Design.* London: Thames and Hudson, 2002.

Lidwell, William, Kritina Holden, and Jill Butler. *Universal Principles of Design.* Gloucester, Mass.: Rockport Publishers, 2003.

Lohse, Richard Paul. *Richard Paul Lohse: Konstruktive Gebrauchsgrafik.* Ostfildern-Ruit, Germany: Hatje Cantz Verlag, 2000.

Müller-Brockmann, Josef. *The Graphic Artist and his Design Problems.* Switzerland: Arthur Niggli Ltd., 1961.

———. *Grid Systems in Graphic Design.* Switzerland: Ram Publications, 1996. First published in 1961.

———. *A History of Graphic Communication.* Switzerland: Arthur Niggli Ltd., 1971.

Murray, Janet. *Hamlet on the Holodeck: The Future of Narrative in Cyberspace.* Cambridge: MIT Press, 1997. 185.

Roberts, Lucienne, and Julia Shrift. *The Designer and the Grid.* East Sussex, UK: RotoVision, 2002.

Rothschild, Deborah, Ellen Lupton, and Darra Goldstein. *Graphic Design in the Mechanical Age: Selections from the Merrill C. Berman Collection.* New Haven: Yale University Press, 1999.

Ruder, Emil. *Typography.* Switzerland: Arthur Niggli Ltd., and New York: Hastings House, 1981. First published in 1967.

Rüegg, Ruedi. *Basic Typography: Design with Letters.* New York: Van Nostrand Reinhold, 1989.

Samara, Timothy. *Making and Breaking the Grid: A Graphic Design Layout Workshop.* Gloucester, Mass.: Rockport Publishers, 2002.

Tufte, Edward R. *Envisioning Information.* Cheshire, Conn.: Graphics Press, 1990.

———. *The Cognitive Style of PowerPoint.* Cheshire, Conn.: Graphics Press, 2003.

MANUALS AND MONOGRAPHS

Alpine, Rachel. *Web Word Wizardry: A Guide to Writing for the Web and Intranet.* Berkeley: Ten Speed Press, 2001.

Baines, Phil, and Andrew Haslam. *Type and Typography.* New York: Watson-Guptill Publications, 2002.

Blackwell, Lewis, and David Carson. *The End of Print: The Grafik Design of David Carson.* San Francisco: Chronicle Books, 2000.

Bringhurst, Robert. *The Elements of Typographic Style.* Vancouver: Hartley and Marks, 1992, 1997.

The Chicago Manual of Style, 15th Edition. Chicago: University of Chicago Press, 2003.

Dwiggins, W. A. *Layout in Advertising.* New York: Harper and Brothers Publishers, 1928.

Eckersley, Richard et al. *Glossary of Typesetting Terms.* Chicago: University of Chicago Press, 1994.

Jury, David. *About Face: Reviving the Rules of Typography.* East Sussex, UK: RotoVision, 2001.

Kane, John. *A Type Primer.* London: Laurence King, 2002.

Kunz, Willi. *Typography: Macro- and Micro-Aesthetics.* Sulgen, Switzerland: Verlag Niggli, 1998.

Lupton, Ellen and J. Abbott Miller. *Design Writing Research: Writing on Graphic Design.* New York: Kiosk, 1996, and London: Phaidon, 1999.

Lynch, Patrick, and Sarah Horton. *Web Style Guide: Basic Design Principles for Creating Web Sites.* New Haven: Yale University Press, 2001.

Newark, Quentin. *What is Graphic Design?* East Sussex, UK: RotoVision, 2002.

Scher, Paula. *Make It Bigger.* New York: Princeton Architectural Press, 2002.

Smith, Ken. *Junk English.* New York: Blast Books, 2001.

Spiekermann, Erik, and E. M. Ginger. *Stop Stealing Sheep and Find Out How Type Works.* Mountain View, Cal.: Adobe Press, 1993.

Strizver, Ilene. *Type Rules: The Designer's Guide to Professional Typography.* Cincinnati: North Light Books, 2001.

Williams, Robin. *The Non-Designer's Design Book: Design and Typographic Principles for the Visual Novice.* Berkeley, Cal.: Peachpit Press, 1994.

———, and John Tollett and David Rohr. *Web Design Workshop.* Berkeley, Cal.: Peachpit Press, 2002.

1792 174